LEARNING THE WAY, THE TRUTH, AND THE LIFE

A JOURNEY OF FAITH

DR. JIM MCCLINTON

WESTBOW
PRESS®
A DIVISION OF THOMAS NELSON
& ZONDERVAN

WestBow Press books may be ordered through booksellers or by contacting:

WestBow Press
A Division of Thomas Nelson & Zondervan
1663 Liberty Drive
Bloomington, IN 47403
www.westbowpress.com
1 (866) 928-1240

ISBN: 978-1-9736-8885-3 (sc)
ISBN: 978-1-9736-8884-6 (e)

Print information available on the last page.

WestBow Press rev. date: 03/20/2020

CONTENTS

PREFACE

First, I thank God for this opportunity to serve and to be an obedient servant to the Spirit. I've prayed that these Messages are a spiritual blessing to some, most, if not all of you who are my brothers and sisters in Christ Jesus. It truly is a blessing to me as well. As you began reading the messages within this book, I believe you'll get to know Christ much better. It's all about Jesus, The Christ! So, please, get to know Christ and not just of Him or about Him. Many who make the claim only know of Him or about Him, and not honestly and spiritually know Him. We do have a choice to do so… to know of Him or to personally Know Him. We can play church or we can be the Church; be religious or be righteous, and so on… Don't take the Joy of salvation for granted. Let's not miss represent our lives or Christ. As a member of the body, let's strive towards "Keeping it Real" with our spiritual journey towards Salvation and Eternal Life. Again, get to Know Christ and not just know of Him. Trust and follow Him! I guarantee this book will help.

For many years, and through much guided preparation, I present this book. With the assistance and counsel of the Holy Spirit, and in obedience, I've been endowed with its power to write this book. Several biblical scriptures have inspired me with their spiritual messages thereof. Not to mention support from my wife, family and friends encouraging me to do so. The following scriptures that have inspired and uplifted me were:

Hosea 4:6 (KJV), "My people are destroyed for lack of knowledge: because thou hast rejected knowledge, I will also reject thee, that thou shalt be no priest to me: seeing thou hast forgotten the law of thy God, I will also forget thy children."

2 Peter 3:18 (KJV), "But grow in grace, and in the knowledge of our Lord and Saviour Jesus Christ. To him be glory both now and forever. Amen."

And lastly, I realized that in order to grow, I had to study; so I was uplifted by: *2 Timothy 2:15* (KJV), "Study to shew thyself approved unto God, a workman that needeth not to be ashamed, rightly dividing the word of truth."

These three scriptures listed above are the fuel and sole reasoning for constructing (writing) these spiritual messages; thus, this book. As mentioned, I've prayed that most, if not all of these Spiritual Messages I've written touch and uplift each reader in a loving spiritual way; of course, depending on the content of each message and what each reader is going through at that time, is how it will spiritually affect each who reads them. I pray it is well with their soul. "God Loves You" and "So Do I." Thank you for acquiring this book. Now, be blessed and while you're being blessed, be a blessing to someone! You don't have to know them or love them, just blessed them as you would want to be blessed. Join with me now in worship, ♪♪♩*"Praise God, from whom all blessings flow!"* I thank God and I thank you! Again, enjoy the book!

AGAPE LOVE

MANY OF US have heard someone say that "All You Need is Love." We've also heard that "Love Makes The World Go Round." Some of us believe that love is essentially important in our lives. It's unfortunate that many don't or have never experienced true love. The New Testament uses the Greek word Agape to refer to God's love. Agape love is the highest form of love. God is love. Perfect Love! (1 Corinthians 13:1-8 NIV). God's definition of agape love is:

"Love is patient." It is long-suffering. It doesn't have a quick temper.

"Love is kind." It shows an authentic interest in others and wants to be upright with others.

"It does not envy." It trusts others and has faith in them.

"It does not boast." It doesn't brag or crow about personal accomplishment or accolades.

"It is not proud." There's no ego.

"It does not dishonor others." It's respectful and considerate of others at all times.

"It is not self-seeking." Others are a priority. It doesn't care about personal gain.

"It is not easily angered." It's slow to speak and swift to hear.

"It keeps no record of wrongs." There's no remembrance of the past and doesn't hold grudges.

"Love does not delight in evil but rejoices with the truth." It thrives on good and just.

"It always protects, always trusts, always hopes, and always perseveres." It is always caring for others. No, *"Love never fails."* Neither does it falter.

Love is the giving of oneself for the benefit of others (John 3:16 KJV); (Romans 5:8 KJV). So, what is love? I would define it this way: JESUS! In John 15:13 (ESV), Jesus declared: "Greater love has no one than this that someone lay down his life for his friends." Jesus made the supreme sacrifice. It was the ultimate expression of love.

We heard Jesus said, in John 13:34-35 (AKJV): "A new command I give you: Love one another. As I have loved you, so you must love one another. By this all men will know that you are my disciples, if you love one another."

God loves all His creation. He is Alpha and Omega. God created this world so Man and all living things would live on it. God loves us and He has a plan for each of our lives. Are we in His plan? Oh yes, we call ourselves having plans too. Whose plan is winning? Whose plan is more predictable? Our plan is not guaranteed! Yes, hard times will come, so that we can learn and appreciate the good times. So we can bend our knees. So, let's love our brothers and sisters all and let's live our best life. The life God intended for us to live. Paul said: "To Live Is Christ to Die Is Gain" Now, let's live for Christ!

We all know that it's easy to say you love someone. Those words just roll off of our tongues. Saying you love someone and truly meaning it or showing it is another matter. Love is an action word, a verb and a noun. I love the word action because action speaks louder than any words. Those of us who Truly LOVE the Lord our actions Verifies it, our action Validates it, our action Justifies it and our action is a witness to our testimony. The Father showed us Love by sending His Son (John 3:16, KJV); Jesus showed us Love by giving His life on the cross; then, He sent/gave us a Gift (The Holy Spirit)... Now, that's Love! That's Agape Love! Yes, the Trinity showed us they Loved us and how much they Loved us. What are we showing them? Rhetorically, ask yourselves: "What Am I Showing Them?" My answer to you is just two words, Follow Christ!

In the scriptures of Ephesians 3:17-19 (NIV), it relates the love of Christ to the knowledge of Christ and considers loving Christ to be a necessity for knowing Him (and not just of Him). We love Him, because He first loved us. Ephesians 5:25 (KJV) states *Christ also loved the church, and gave Himself up for it*. Now, Jesus has given us a commandment to "Love one another, as He has loved us (John 13:34, KJV)... A word of love gives spice to life. Remember, a happy and successful life begins with God and ends for God. Yawl have a safe, prayerful, loving and Godly life! Tell someone, somewhere that you love them and mean it. God/Jesus is Love! I love yawl, in Jesus Name!

We all religiously proclaim the word LOVE. A 1984 song by British-American rock band Foreigner, asked: ♪♪"I Want to Know What LOVE Is." It's been shared in a movie and also a song that: ♪♪"LOVE is a Many Splendored Things." American icon, singer, actress, and television show host Dionne Warwick in 1960 shared: ♪♪"What the World Needs Now is LOVE Sweet LOVE". In 1980, R&B group The Whispers told us that, ♪♪"It's a LOVE Thing". Lastly, in 1960, Deon Jackson enlightens us that: ♪♪"LOVE Makes the World Go Round." For sure, LOVE is very essential. Do you agree?

There is a LOVE we all should want and showcase called 'AGAPE LOVE', I mentioned it in an earlier message. This kind of LOVE is given and shared not because of, but in spite of. God (John 3:16, KJV) gave His Son; Son gave His life; then, Son sent/gave us as a gift - The Holy Spirit. Now that's a whole lot of LOVE. As Believers, we should express the same type of LOVE that God/Jesus has shown and is still showing towards us. No! I'm not talking about Puppy LOVE or Brotherly LOVE (smile). If we really and seriously want to know what True Unconditional LOVE is, we should get to know Jesus! Jesus is LOVE. Oh yes He is! I conclude with: American singer, songwriter, actor, and record producer, Lionel Richie and

The Commodores" ♪♪♪"Jesus Is LOVE" Speaking for myself, ♪♪♪"I'm in LOVE with Jesus, and He's in LOVE with me" By the way, I LOVE Yawl!

Now someone is asking, 'if I Love,' "What's in it for me?" Is being commanded to Love enough? We are blessed to bless others. We are loved to love others. In Matthew 22:37-39 (KJV) Jesus said, "you shall Love the Lord your God with all your heart, with all your soul, and with all your mind." This is the first and great commandment. And the second is like it: 'You shall Love your neighbor as yourself.'" Who's obedient to these two great commandments? God blessed us with a beautiful musical genius and artist, Patti LaBelle asking: ♪♪♪ "What Can I Do For You"♪ Here's a few verses to comprehend...

> ♪♪♪"People want to live - Not merely exist
> People want to enjoy - Not suffer and fear
> People need understanding - Not tensions or confusion
> Oh I wonder should the people who present us this solution talk about Love
> Love Love
> Love Love Love - Love Love Love ♪ So, can someone tell me?
> "What Can I Do For You?" - "What Can You Do For Me?" Love! Love! Love!"

Family, it's our nature to always want something. Who want to serve? We're supposed to be servants! But the question is always – I want, I want, I want... Is there anyone who prefers giving? Someone somewhere said that "it's better to give than to receive." Okay, who's giving Love? Some of us might recall a 1965 popular song by Jackie DeShannon, "What the World Needs Now (is love, sweet love)." Yes, the world, you and I (We) need Love! Did you know that it is critical to our salvation that we know the value and the importance of Love? Love is the key to all we do in our Christian life. It is the key to our ministry; the key to our relationships; and the key to our eternal life. We're reminded in 1 Corinthians 13:2 NIV, "If I have the gift of prophecy and can fathom all mysteries and all knowledge, and if I have a faith that can move mountains, but do not have love, I am nothing." So, without LOVE, what do we have? NOTHING! Also, Matthew 5:8 KJV says, "Blessed are the pure in heart: for they shall see God." And, 1 Peter 1:22 KJV tells us to: "love one another with a pure heart fervently" I Love Yawl!

What do we know about love? What do we know about God's love? God's love knows no bounds. In 2 Corinthians 13:11 (KJV), the Apostle Paul described God as one of "love and peace." For us to feel His love, this same love He has, we need to show love to others. "Thou shalt love thy neighbor as thyself" (Matthew 22:39, KJV). No way am I singing my own praises... I Love the Lord!

I'm curious! Do we truly know what Love is? "Jesus loves us this ----------------MUCH!"

Sometimes some of us don't feel Loved, or we don't feel worthy of Love. Sin interferes with all our relationships, especially the one relationship we need to have with God. In Ephesians 3:18-19 (NIV), Apostle Paul's prayer was that we would "… grasp how wide and long and high and deep, and thus to know the love of Christ that surpasses knowledge, so that we may be filled up to the measure of all the fullness of God." God has our best interest in mind. Paul also tells us in Romans 5:8 (NIV), "… God demonstrates His own Love for us in this: While we were still sinners, Christ died for us."

One of the most vivid characteristics of God is that He is a God of Love. God's Love is shown through salvation, forgiveness and restoration. Scripture also say, "And we have come to know and to believe the Love that God has for us. Whoever lives in love lives in God and God lives in them" (1 John 4:16, NIV). As we ponder the love of Christ for us, and the different ways that the Bible presents it to us, we begin to understand how the depth of Christs' (JESUS') Love is revealed! Yes, Jesus Loves us and gave Himself up for us, an offering and a sacrifice. That was how much He loved us! Today, even now, Jesus still loves us. Family, can you feel the Love? Do you know and can you personally say: "Jesus Loves ME this------------------MUCH?" Now, ♪♪"Say You Love Him" (Rev. James Cleveland, 1976). ♪♪"Dear Jesus I Love You" (Walter Hawkins, 1975).

GROWING IN GRACE

ONE OF MY utmost and favorite scriptures is 2 Peter 3:18 (KJV). Although I wrote these Spiritual Messages, it wasn't me, I was led spiritually. No, it's not about me; it's about He that is within me. I write because of Him. I write because there is a need… In Hosea 4:6 (KJV), it tells us that God's people are being destroyed for lack of knowledge. I feel, and I know I've been chosen, shaped, molded and now responsible towards helping believers who want to grow in grace and in the knowledge of our Lord and Savior Jesus the Christ. (I know I have some Soldiers out there like me.)

Every Sunday denominational churches have members that are not being fed the word; in some instances, they are not being led by the Holy Spirit. They are what my wife and I would call *Fidgets*; they barely move. They don't grow they just idle. I've been in a church like that; maybe, someone is still in that church… Of course, this does not apply to every local church. Some Ministers and Pastors do a God-Pleasing job in the spiritual growth of their parishioners. We as believers want to grow in the Lord. We want to learn, grow and know the Gospel, contrary to those who want to talk the Gossip. I love it when I hear a minister preach the gospel and not just about the gospel. My prayer is for all receiving these messages Learn, Know, and Grow in the Word and to follow Christ, while being led by the Holy Spirit. Am I asking too much?

As we "Grow in Grace and in the Knowledge of our Lord and our Savior" (2 Peter 3:18 KJV), Satan is present, waiting to pounce. It is very important to understand who our adversary the Devil is, and what he is able to do. But God is standing by… We must be vigilante, understanding that as our Faith grows from one level to the next, and the adversary is still present. No, he hasn't gone anywhere and he is still on the prowl; did someone say, "Every level there's another devil?"? Let us pray continuously and stay in the word, keeping Satan at bay. ♪♫"STOMP on the devils head" Remember, God has you. Do you have Him? Let's Grow…

Omnipotence means God is all-powerful. God has supreme power and has no limitations (none). Omniscience means God is all-knowing. God knows everything, including our past and our future (yes He does). Omnipresence means God is everywhere. God is present everywhere in His creation (us/the world), but distinct from it. God is here right now, as you read this message. Can you feel Him? It's a blessing and an encouragement for Believers (us) to Fellowship with God. If God is only in heaven - we might ask, "How can I commune with

Him?" It doesn't matter if we are here in the USA, in China, Hawaii, Poland, Mexico, in a Cathedral, a jail or a poor ghetto house, we can fellowship with God anywhere! Yes, He's All-Powerful, All-Knowing, and Everywhere! Can you feel Him? I don't know about you, but He's My Everything, My Omni (all). My All! Is He Yours?

Some, as I, is fortunately blessed and highly favored to have been chosen, shaped and molded to teach and share Gods word, going on many years now. I, as you are fortunate and blessed to have allowed God to humble, mold and use me as He saw fit; and, as He's still doing presently. Encouraged by God's Salvation, it's been my pleasure and an honor to study (2 Timothy 2:15 KJV), and to Grow in Grace (2 Peter 3:18 KJV); that I've lived, so God could use me. Knowing that the continued ongoing studying of God's Word through bible studies, Sunday/Church School, Prayer Meetings, and Prayer Lines were not at all in vain. God's purpose, preparing me for 'His Will be done' - God in me and through me. We've been told to be careful of what we ask for, and "ask and you shall receive."

I've asked that God Endow Me with the Power of the Holy Spirit, to be led to do His Will. To some, if it applies, STUDY, GROW, stay PRAYED UP. Humble yourselves and make yourselves available to allow Him to use you; someway, somehow; His Way! We need to get ready, be ready and stay ready for God to use each of us! We're on His time, not ours. None of us like to be used - God is the exception. Let's Do This! Just ask Him, "Use Me Lord?"

Do any of us wonder why God allows the storms to enter/embark into our lives? I've heard someone say "God often puts us in situations that are too much for us to handle so that we will learn that no situation is too much for Him." I've also heard that "God won't put on us no more than we can bear." Know that He got you. Yes, He Got Us! Can you say that the Lord is your Helper? Do you know the Lord? Are you His Child? Can you call out to Him in prayer? Does He keep you from stumbling? Does He give you strength each day? Is the Lord watching over you? Does the Lord deliver you in your trials and tribulations? Is He leading you towards Paradise? Does your confidence rest in Him? What is your Hope built on? God knows each of us personally, and He and only He will never let you be tempted more than you can bear. Again, He Got You!

I believe we all want to be what God would have us to be. He wants us to exhibit His Characteristics: "The Fruits of the Spirit" in our life's journey. In Galatians 5:22-23 (NIV), the fruit of the Spirit of God is "love, joy, peace, patience, kindness, goodness, faithfulness, gentleness, and self-control"... Collectively, these Fruits are nine visible attributes all of us should be producing. As a Believer, we must "bear much fruit," because Christ uses each of us to bring about blessed, celestial results in a fallen world. "Bearing Fruit" is a Biblical concept used to describe the thoughts, words, and deeds produced by someone's soul. For us to obtain eternal life, a soul must prove it has repented of sin by bearing the Good Fruit of Love. Jesus used symbolism of the Grape Vine to illustrate our relationship with God. Yes, Jesus is the Vine; His disciples (Us) are the branches, and God the Father is the Vinedresser. "The fruit of the righteous is a tree of life" (Proverbs 11:30, KJV). Okay, Tree branches bear fruit! Jesus says: "I am the Vine, ye are the branches: He that abideth in me, and I in him the same bringeth forth much fruit (John 15:4-11, KJV).

Biblically, the metaphor of fruit describes the produce of our lives. Another metaphor uses God the Father as the gardener (John 15:1, KJV), and He desires each of us to be fruitful. Our God has planted the seed (Jesus) of Life in us; we've grown in Grace (branches), now let us branch out and bear Spiritual Fruit, someone somewhere is hungry and our tree is the closest tree to them. Feed them, give them fruit!

Daily, we (you/I) face evils (sin) not understanding our own actions. God hates sin because it is contrary to the righteous, purity, and holy nature of God. Because of our sinful nature, our sinful flesh inevitable remains within us, and we all struggle ethically in every imaginable aspect known; at least, some of us. Do we have or want the desire to do what is right? There is a great battle being waged within us (Spirit vs. flesh). Paul speaks in Romans 7:15-20 (NIV) of this struggle when he says, "For I do not do what I want, but I do the very thing I hate... For I have the desire to do what is right, but not the ability to carry it out. For I do not do the good I want, but the evil I do not want is what I keep on doing." Let us live by the Spirit because God's Grace is all-sufficient.

Unfortunately, Someone, Somebody, Somewhere feel that the sacrifices they're making for the Lord is a waste of time. Recently, some questionable thoughts crossed my mind - maybe they've crossed yours too. These same pondering thoughts and questions, each of us has to answer for ourselves; just as King Solomon and the Apostle Paul asked... "Is our praying, singing, preaching, teaching, praising, worshiping, giving, communion, fasting, hardships, internal suffering with the Thorn in our sides – is it all in vain?" And, have we wasted our time? "Therefore, my beloved brethren, be steadfast, immovable, always abounding in the work of the Lord, – knowing that your labor is not in vain in the Lord" (1Corinthians 15:58, ESV). What makes our good work good isn't our intent, it isn't about us, it never has been; rather, what makes our work good is when it's about/for the Lord! Unless we invite and partner with God in Christ in whatever we are saying, doing, or participating in – it is in vain. So, don't be discouraged, be encouraged and be strong in the Lord and in the power of His might. Let us continue to spread the Word (Gospel) that when we see the fruit of the Spirit building up in us (You/Me) and/or around us...we can rejoice and it not be in vain (Psalm 127:1-2, NIV)... To all who is reading this particular message and the blessings that derives from it – know that it's not in vain. Certainly, God's Love and My Love for each of you is not in vain.

Times are hard; I, as many of you have experienced personal HARDSHIP. What would our life in Christ be without HARDSHIP? Scripture tells us that we would have Trials and Tribulations. As Believers, when we put our faith in Jesus, we're declaring war against Satan. When we pledge our allegiance to Christ, we have already taken a stand with God and against the devil, with the truth and against sin. Now the devil is not happy at what he is seeing. This is when the Hardships of Trials and Tribulations manifest. Paul in 2 Timothy 2:3, NIV tells us to: "Endure hardship, as a good soldier of Jesus Christ." So, it's important that we have this perspective, and be mentally prepared for these Hardships. I'm not saying it will be easy... NO, our belief in Christ does not immune us from the hardships of life. Yes, life can be very dark and hard on us but we must learn to see/live it in the LIGHT (Jesus). Okay, we've established that there will be hardships and sufferings. 2 Corinthians 5:4 KJV says; "For while we are in this tent, we groan and are burdened..."

Trials and Hardships strengthen our faith and develop perseverance. We become more spiritual mature and complete in Christ because of them, and not apart from them. Simply, we are better off having Hardships, than not having Hardships (James 1:2, KJV). Apostle Paul did not merely endure his hardships. He gloried in them, can we? Inevitably, scripture tells us we will experience Trials and Hardships but it's our (yours and mine) choice that they NOT separate or drive a wedge between Me/You and God, or My/Our love for Christ (Romans 8:35, KJV). "Finally, my Brothers and Sisters), through all the hard times), Yawl be strong in the Lord, and in the power of His might."

Do any of you remember these classic songs? ♪♪"I Can't Get No Satisfaction" ♪♪"Satisfaction Guaranteed or Take Your Love Back" Yes, Satisfaction means one's fulfillment, wishes, needs or expectations; and/or the payment of a debt. You know Jesus paid it all and all to Him we owe. Now, are we satisfied with where we are - where we need to be in Christ? The answer should be NO! I've gotten some spiritual Satisfaction, but I'm Not Satisfied with where I am or where I need to be in Christ Jesus. Are you? I want to be endowed with the power of the Holy Spirit more and to get closer to Him and In Him. I want to be Wrapped Up, Tied Up, and Tangled Up in Him- daily. Yawl be blessed and please, don't be Satisfied with where you are in Christ - Get Closer! Grow!!!

Is it just me or have some of you ever woken up wanting to just talk to the Lord? Someone sang: ♪♪"Just a Closer Walk with Thee" Myself, ♪♪"I want to walk and talk with Jesus each and every day; I want my life to be an example for Him in every way. I want to treat my brothers and sisters the way that He wants me to; because He said, Do unto others as you would have them to do unto you; I want Him to shower me with His blessings from up above and rock me, rock me, rock me in the cradle of His love..." Okay, I don't think it's just me!

Some time ago, it came to my attention that Spiritual Messages like these are only for 'babes' in Christ. If so, is that a bad thing? Many of us may have been 'babes' in Christ at one time, some of us may be 'babes' in Christ right now - but we don't have to stay one. We grow as our faith grows. Truth is; we all need the Word of God daily. Yes, our spiritual growth is our personal responsibility of having a personal relationship with Christ. Our primary goal in life should be to become more like Jesus Christ. If we're to wear His holy name (CHRISTian) and if we are Believers then we should live a life that is worthy of His name.

There are those of us who desire the Word, like 'babes', desire and have a longing for the pure milk of the Word. Scriptures tells us that the sincere (pure) milk of the Word is a must, if one is to grow (1 Peter 2:2, KJV). Does that mean we're all 'babes' in Christ? NO! Jesus said, "He who is of God hears (obeys) the words of God." And David (Psalm 119:72, KJV) said, "The Word of God is more desirable than gold..." It's good to acknowledge that what feeds 'babes' first - is the Word and we thank God for giving it (the Word) to us. As we ('babes') "Grow in Grace and Knowledge" of the Word, let us reaffirm our longing, and our desire for it, that we might continuously grow into spiritual maturity (the meat) as mature adults of the word; thus, bringing God the Glory. There will always be 'babes' in the Member of the Body of Christ. Prayerfully, at some point in their Spiritual-Christian journey, they will be weaned off milk (as 'babes') unto the meat (as mature adults) in the word, spiritually. No matter which or who we are, 'babes' or adults, we all need the Word of God, continuously, daily and without limitations because "the word of the Lord endures forever." (Peter 1:25, KJV) I Love Milk... Got Milk???

Blessings come in many forms. God has blessed each of us with many different gifts, in many different ways, for many different purposes. What is sure and certain beyond any doubt is that God has blessed each of us. We belong to Him. Now, can each of us personally count our blessings? Are there many; those we know of, and those we know not of? Are we owed them, or, do we deserve them? Are there any witnesses that are ♪♫"Blessed and Highly Favored" (Clark Sisters)? Any witnesses that we are too blessed to be depressed; that we are blessed in our coming in and blessed in our going out. God's blessings are not just filling our cup, but spilling it over. When our cup overflows, (with blessings), it shows us how much God wants us to stay with Him and enjoy being with Him; and, Him giving Him the Glory! No, we don't have to manipulate or coerce God for Him to approve of us or bless us. Or, to show us Favor!

In fact, He gives Himself to us, the ultimate blessing. We are blessed, but only blessed through Christ. You know our blessings from God are so much more than merely our material possessions, needs and wants. God blesses us so that we can live our lives in such a way that the people around us can see HIM. Only Him! He blesses us so that we can be a blessing. Musical icon Charlie Wilson sings: "I'm Blessed" and Gospel Legends The Clark Sister's song also verifies: ♪♫"I Am Blessed." So, I Know we (you and I) are truly blessed because ♪♫"The Lord is blessing me, right now, oh, right now!" Now ask yourselves, "Am I blessing someone?" "Am I a blessing to someone?" Are You? In Jesus' Name, Yawl be blessed!

Because we are greatly distressed, have any of us ever felt that we can't win our battles on our own? The devil is a deceiver and a liar; he is always scheming against those of us who accept and follow Christ. If he's not scheming against you, he already has you. He knows our weakness and will seek to exploit them. Like David, while at his weakest, he was unable to fight in his own strength until he realize he could "be strong in the Lord and in the strength of His might" (Ephesians 6:10, KJV). We should always remember that "The joy of the Lord is our strength" (Nehemiah 8:10, KJV). God is saying to each of us: "Have I not commanded you - be strong and courageous? Do not be frightened, and do not be dismayed, for the Lord your God is with you wherever you go" (Joshua 1.9, KJV). Besides, Jesus has already overcome this world for (us) the redeemed, and nothing or no one can defeat Him; (Colossians 2:15, KJV). Yes, we can win! Remember: "But thanks be to God who gives us the victory through our Lord Jesus Christ" (1 Corinthians 15:57, KJV). Anyone still distressed?

Oh what a joy it is to be forgiven and to be born again; knowing that "Jesus the author and finisher of our faith" (Hebrews 12:2). Yes, He is definitely the author of our Salvation! Acts 4:12 (NIV) tells us that Salvation is in Him alone. "Jesus said to him, "I am the way, and the truth, and the life. No one comes to the Father except through me" - John 14:6 (ESV). Now that's something to praise about! I can hear Mahalia Jackson singing: ♪♪"Come to Jesus, Come to Jesus, Come to Jesus just now?" Oh what great joy!

I've been in deep thought about being religious and/or not being religious enough - but having 'That Old Time Religion.' Few of you might authentically remember 'That Old Time Religion.' Though, each of our personal perceptions might've been 'our favorite preacher;' 'our favorite songs;' 'our favorite home church;' and/or, other memorable things. I believe the obvious thing we've forgotten is what made our memories of that time authentic. What made that 'Old Time Religion' so great was our enormous faith and commitment of a generation now past. As a Baby Boomer myself, and even those that came before me, we depended on God, spent time in His word, loved/treated others like we wanted to be loved/treated, and had a strong Faith in God and a relationship with Christ. God was indeed the answer for all of our situations. They/We lived out what they/we believed.

We had a strong family unit, strong morals, values, and strong culture; not to mention a strong country. "Under God" was not simply two words in the Pledge of Allegiance, it was their/our way of life! "In God We Trust" wasn't just four words on our money, we seriously and spiritually trusted Him. Prayer in schools wasn't a pastime; it was our Faith in action. We "Train up a child in the way he should go" (Proverbs 22:6, KJV). Yes, that 'Old Time Religion' was a lifestyle. It was integrated in every part of their/our lives. No, they/we weren't perfect; they/we just possessed a sincere and deep understanding of what it meant to daily love and live for Christ - in Christ. This is that 'Old Time Religion' I, and some of you might remember.

At some point and somewhere along the way, "going to church" instead of "being the church" took precedence. Possibly, the message of the Gospel was eventually replaced with carnal and worldly gossip; which unfortunately, kept the church body in turmoil, even to this day. Thus, the 'local Church' changed... I know some have said we have to change because of the times but I serve a Savior who never changes and neither do His principles. God is the same yesterday and today!

There was a time when almost every preacher preached the Word, but now some; if not most are doing is competing with the world, pleasing man, or self. That wasn't Gods intention. So we don't preach or teach like we use to, we just create and have programs. I am challenged to personally examine myself and I challenge others to make sure the "Old Time Religion" is preached and taught like when I was a boy and even way before me - was the same. Back then they preached and taught the gospel; and not about the gospel, but The Gospel of the Living Christ. The Gospel According to Jesus Christ! The Good News! It benefitted the same results as back then. I Pray that God ♪♪"Give Me That Old Time Religion! Hallelujah it'll be good enough for me!" Definitely, the world wants and needs a religion with salvation in it. If you are not into that 'Old Time Religion' and you just can't clamor it, seek the New Covenant relationship with the bridegroom, Jesus Christ, and the bride, His church (us), which is the same. Yes, "Gimme that old time religion, it's good enough for me!" Is it good enough for you? ♪♪"To God Be The Glory!"

Do we value HOPE the way God intends for us to? Is our HOPE positive, inspiring and powerful? Most of us understand that life without HOPE is empty. But what is real HOPE in life for Believers like you and me? True hope is a uniquely Christian thing like faith and love. King David wrote, "You are my HOPE, O Lord GOD" and "I HOPE in Your Word" (Psalm 71:5 & Psalm 119:147, KJVs). The Apostle Paul said we are urged as Christians "to lay hold of the HOPE set before us" (Titus 1:2; 2:13, KJV). I believe we all wonder how we can have HOPE when everything that is going on today looks HOPEless. NO, our circumstances of today may not change, but God can change us in the midst of them. Yes, Our HOPE is in God's love not our circumstances.

Our HOPE is not in a crisis, it is in the crucified Christ, and the empty tomb. God is looking for those of us who aren't looking to our circumstances, but to Him for HOPE. Back in the day, activist Jessie Jackson told us to "Keep HOPE Alive!" We need to be motivated by this same HOPE today! You and I (we) have no HOPE of being in God's Kingdom or of being in a relationship with Him, except by being as righteous as Christ. F.Y.I. ♪♪"My HOPE is built on nothing less, than Jesus' blood and righteousness..." Psalm 39:7, KJV says: "And now, Lord, what wait I for? My HOPE is in thee." Romans 15:13, ESV says: "May the God of HOPE fill you with all joy and peace in believing, so that by the power of the Holy Spirit you may abound in HOPE." Yes, we are a people of HOPE! My HOPE for us today, is to allow God to continue building something in each of us that He, others, and each of us will be proud of. I'm HOPEful, are You?

Man has a natural desire in his heart to please God. To fulfill this innate desire, many attempt to serve Him in their own ways, not His. Just doing what we think or feel, or what a denomination or religion says to do, is "religious" and it does not make one RIGHT before God. We all grew up and was taught to do what's RIGHT; most of us grew up into some type of RELIGIOUS denominational life. There's a difference between being RELIGIOUS and being RIGHTEOUS. One is traditional, pleasing self and man; the other is led by the Holy Spirit, pleasing God. "Religion" is mentioned only 5-7 times, in the King James Version; whereas, "Righteous" is mentioned 238-300+times. Go figure... There were many "religious" people in the Bible (Nicodemus, Pharisees...) that even Christ knew were not RIGHTEOUS.

There are some, if not many existing among us today. I pray none of us are in that number. We have a choice to choose between being Religious and being RIGHTEOUS. Just remember this; God our Father highly favors His RIGHTEOUS saints. Did someone say: "Only the righteous shall see God"? "For the Lord is righteous, He loves justice; upright men will see His face" (Psalm 11:7, KJV). "Blessed are the pure in heart, for they will see God" (Matthew 5:8, NIV). Also, check out King James Versions of: (Proverbs 21:21 * Psalm 34:15 * 1 Timothy 6:11 * James 5:16 * 2 Corinthians 5:21) I Love You!

Some of us may be, or some of us may not be aware that something is separating us from God, from His presence... Possibly, something or someone; no matter how small it may be it is separating us from the Lord and His Love thereof. Is it money, family, tradition, religion, sex, hatred, malice, politics, social media, cell phones, or anyone? Whatever it is, it's blocking our blessing and our Favor of God. We'd like to give God 100% of our attention; not 50%, 75%, 30%, and most definitely not 99 ½% because even that won't do. Everything gets our undivided attention 100% of the time; why can't God? Tithing only asks for 10%; whereas, God request and deserves 100% of our time if we are true Believers, Followers, Christians of the Gospel (Him). This message is for Me/You/Us! If toes are stepped on, draw them up... Something or Someone is separating me - of not being 100% attentive to My God, My Savior, My Lord, My Jesus and My Salvation. Personally, I need to find out what it is and get right (100%) with God and do it now (John 9:4, KJV). Maybe; just maybe, I'm the only one, in this predicament. Please excuse me, I have work to do, My Salvation is on the line. I pray that God grants each of you100% Blessings!

Some, if not a lot of us are hooked on something; self, or maybe someone. I'm not talking about a habit. Being HOOKED is defined as being very interested and enthusiastic about (something). It's not an issue to be hooked, it depends... Someone may be hooked on chocolate, material things, his or her cell phones, Facebook, eating certain foods; God forbid drugs, alcohol, sex, lying, or any other negative vices. I'm not judging because I have my own personal hooks. And NO, I'm not hooked on Phonics (anymore) (smile). Seriously, I am hooked on The Father, The Son and The Holy Ghost! Anyone else hooked on The Trinity? Any of us; anyone, at any time can get hooked. And when we are hooked by Jesus, it's only a matter of time before we are Hooked on Jesus. Being hooked on Jesus means making an adult-mature commitment to a life of service (servanthood), and a life of praise and worship to God (it's your choice). Yes, in turn, God surely will "hook you up" (Favor). And it's important that we get "hooked" on Jesus. We are to be hooked up, consistently and constantly connected to Christ. Our Soul Salvation depends on it. Now, let's asked this question? Do any of you have "The Hook Up"? Are You Hooked (On Jesus)?

Some of us, if not all of us are daily in the Will of God; we're living so God can continuously use us. Yes, we live; Yes, we're living (in Him)... Did someone say that they were Livin' it Up? Anyway, it's not about just eating, drinking and being merry. As we live, are we living up to God's expectations; His Standards; or, His Characteristics? Are we doing "What Thus Saith The Lord"? Are we being obedient to His Word? Then the question is: "Is My Living In Vain?" "Is my Praying, Laboring, Preaching, Teaching, Singing, Ushering, or Fasting in vain?" I Pray Not! I want nothing to prevent/keep my redeemed name from being blotted out/off the Book of Life (Lamb's Book of Life). God's People (GP), can you feel me? Can I get a witness? Hallelujah!!!

Let's Talk! We've always heard, or biblically been taught that as a Believer, or Christian that we need to have a Personal Relationship with God/Jesus; to not just know of Him but, to Spiritually and Personally Know Him. Communication is an important aspect in every healthy relationship, including our relationship with God. The more we spend time with Him, the more we get to know Him and His love for us. Like in any relationship, one must be able to get to know each other, spend time together and communicate with one another. In other words, both parties must converse with each other, have dialogue; and it's not just a one-sided conversation. Yes; Spouses, Significant Others, Boyfriends or Girlfriends must talk to each other in order to have a good working and healthy relationship.

How's Our Relationship with the Trinity? Are We Communicating With The Father, The Son and The Holy Spirit? We spend a ridiculous amount of time communicating on Social Media Websites, etc.... Has anyone ever been able to Communicate with The Trinity on Facebook, FaceTime, Twitter, Instagram, Myspace, WeChat, Snap Chat, LinkedIn or Texting? Are any of you 'Old School' like me; preferably, going to Our War Room, Prayer Room and/or Closet, get down on our bending knees and humble ourselves before The Trinity; Praying to The Father, in The Spirit, in The Name of Jesus? Communicating - because of Our Relationship! Am I the only one with this type of Relationship? I'm just sayin'... Yawl be blessed! Now please excuse me... ♪♪"I'm Gonna Have A Little Talk With Jesus."

"Confessions" If we are Born Again, then let us not proclaim to be anyone but who we are, as we continuously Hope and Pray to be what God has called and anointed each of us to be (in Him). Some, if not most of us may not be where we need to be in our Faith; or, where we should be; and, where God wants and expect us to be. As we grow in Him (Grace), our Faith grows. Yes, we are definitely still a work in progress. And definitely, He has lots of work yet to do with me! What about you? We must trust our Faith and "Grow In Grace and in the Knowledge of Our Lord, Jesus The Christ" (2 Peter 3:18, NIV). "We Must Lean Not to our own understanding" (Proverbs 3:5, NIV). We must stand on His (Jesus') Word, as we continuously learn of it/Him. We must ask forgiveness and also, forgive. We are loved of Him (God/Jesus), and with our heart and soul, we love Him (Matthew 22:37-39, KJV), as we must love (our neighbor). We must also serve others (man), because we are Servants of God. Well, only 3 words left to say: "Let's Do This?"

Has anyone ever asked themselves: "Where would I be without the Lord?" If not, here's your opportunity! Ask Yourselves: "Where would I be and who would I be?" "Would I be Christ-like, a Believer, a Vessel, and/or the Living Sanctuary God would have me to be?" Honestly, we do know the answer - and definitely God knows. (James 4:13-17, KJV) Let each of us do what we need to do to please God and be in His Will. "If It Is To Be, It's Up To Me!" It's my soul salvation I'm takin' bout... Being self-reliant, relying on one's self is a sin in the sight of God. So, where would I be without the Lord? Myself, I can't even phantom the thought. Can you?

The Lord knows that we've all had our share of life's ups and downs. None of us drama are free. Scriptures tell us we will have trials and tribulations: hardships, drama, sickness, health issues, financial disparities, seen/unseen danger, deaths and bereavement. It also tells us that we would sometimes find ourselves in the valley, in the storm or in the wilderness alone. But He said He'd never leave us nor forsake us... Now, here I am; a witness, a living testimony of who God is and what He can do, if I'm obedient and if I pray. Yes, I pray and thank God that I have been what He has intended me to be. I pray that I've been obedient to the Holy Spirit while constructing this spiritual message. I pray that I have expressed and shown the Agape Love of Christ in all of my sayings, doings and concessions, non-wavering. Not because I have this bully pulpit, and not because I'm physically suffering from some type of illness right now, but because of who's in me. Isaiah 53:5 (KJV) tells us, "But he was wounded for our transgressions, he was bruised for our iniquities: the chastisement of our peace was upon him;

and with His stripes we are healed." And through it all, we continue to stand on His Word. Keep standing, keep believing, keep trusting and keep obeying. Yes, God's got us! I pray that we have Him… No matter our circumstances, I also praying that we continue in love and prayer for one-another, in the name of Jesus. ♪♫"To God Be The Glory!"

For decades, questions have been asked: Why did the Lord choose Judas? Why did the Lord choose Job, Moses, Peter, Paul, Ruth, David or Solomon? Okay, why did the Lord's choose you? Why did He choose me? Why Not Us? Was it because of our unique and imaginative methodology or, our philosophical theology? NO! It was because we were common men and women and we knew the Lord, experiencing His life and His characteristics of Godliness and the power of the Spirit of God. Christ chose us (you and me) for what we were, and what we hope to be, not for what we may become, or have become. We must remember Christ called and chose him (Judas); and God choose Moses, Paul, Peter, Ruth, David, etc... and not in vain; He loved them all, and not without cause. Just as He loves, calls and chooses us. Christ chooses us not for our attainments, but for our possibilities. Yes, ♪♫"I am a promise, I am a possibility

I am a promise with a capital P; I am a great big bundle of potentiality

And I am learnin' to hear God's voice; And I am tryin' to make the right choice

I am a promise to be anything God wants me to be." Yes, a promise I am; and Christ has called and chosen me. Now, rhetorically ask yourselves, has God called and/or chosen me? If not, He still can! He will! Are you listening?

♪♫"It is well, It is well, with my Soul" Is It? ♪♫"My Soul cries out Hallelujah!" Does It? Our Soul Salvation should be the most important thing in life as breathing. Or at least it should be. Yes, Salvation is Free; it's being justified freely by His Grace through the redemption that is in Christ (Romans 3:24, KJV). I, as well as Pastors, Preachers, Teachers and Evangelists all are not Salesmen - we're just bearers of Good News. Isaiah 55:1, NIV said: our Salvation is "without money and without price". We cannot barter with God. He holds in His Omnipotent hand the priceless, precious, eternal gift of Salvation. Yes, the best things in life are free, are they not? Love is free, Faith is free, Hope is free, and Salvation is free. Yawl better get your Gift... Glory Hallelujah!

When we are given heavy loads by God, it only means that we are worthy of His trust. He trusts us to carry them. Trust is not exactly the same as faith, which is the gift of God (Ephesians 2:8-9, KJV). Rather, trusting is what we do because of the faith we have been given. Trusting is believing in the promises of God in all circumstances, even in those where the evidence seems to be to the contrary. Nevertheless, the practical consequence of faith in God is trust, which we prove by living out our full acceptance of God's promises day by day. Let us continue to 'Live on Purpose.' Trust Him!

I'd like to make known that I am very serious about my love for The Trinity and my love for all who are reading these messages. I am also serious about my salvation and my spiritual atmosphere. I pray that all who reads this message are serious as well. Whether we know it or not, if we claim to be His, we are examples. Of course the ultimate example is Christ. As a Christ-like believer (CHRISTian), it allows us to be followers. We must be a mature Christian that someone can model; and by biblical standards, someone who influences others. We can never be what God has called us to be, until we realize God has called us to be examples to others (1 Timothy 4:12, KJV). ♪♪♪"To be like Jesus…" Do any of us want to be like Mike? Now you all know who my example is: who's yours? Yawl be blessed and please, be an example of Christ to someone. And again remember, someone is watching…

We as believers in this Christendom Era are living in serious and dire straits times. We have scriptures that speak of Salvation, Eternal Life, Heaven and Hell, Judgement Day, Righteousness and Unrighteousness. Is there a miracle that God hasn't shown us for us to see that our Salvation is a serious matter? What new spiritual insight do we need to help us get closer to the Lord? Nicodemus' answer wasn't enough, now what else is there for us "to be born again." Are we getting or being endowed with the power of the Holy Spirit? Do we need to become more empowered and clearer on our purpose and our journey in Christ Jesus? We can't continue and we must stop playing Church. We are the Church! Let's not forsake the fellowship of ourselves (Hebrews 10:24-25, KJV). Members of the Body, yawl be blessed!

At some time or another, in each of our lives, we've all been taken advantage of in some form or another. We've been used and abused. In all circumstances, it probably wasn't necessarily all bad; yet, it happens. Questions: Do we use God? Do we take advantage of God? Should we? Believe it or not, God wants to be taken advantage of. And, He wants us to use Him. God gives us many advantages, if only we'd take them. Remember, anything (everything) good in our lives comes from God. James 1:17, KJV tells us, "Every good gift and every perfect gift is from above, and cometh down from the Father…" It is sad to think that something (a blessing) was available for us and we missed out on receiving it. Oh no, you mean you didn't take advantage of your blessing(s)?

It's scary to believe that we can miss out on God's blessings and healings. God wants not just some of our concerns, He want all of them. He wants to bless us concerning all of them, so take advantage of that… We need to act on all the opportunities we have to receive the grace of God in its many forms. Don't hesitate; no matter the circumstances, take advantage of God's Forgiveness, His Grace, His Love, His Mercy, His Favor, His Redemption, and The Holy Spirit. But we should never take God's Goodness for Granted. Never! Please, don't take this message for granted?

The Biblical scripture of 2 Corinthians 10:3-4 NIV says: "For though we live in the world (flesh), we do not wage war as the world (flesh) does. The weapons we fight with are not the weapons of the world (carnal)." On the contrary, they have divine power to demolish strongholds. A stronghold is anything in our lives that is not bringing glory to God.

- ➤ Every lie of the enemy is a stronghold.
- ➤ Anything that is not allowing us to see the truth of God's WORD is a stronghold.
- ➤ Unbelief is a stronghold.
- ➤ Fear is a stronghold.
- ➤ Not trusting in God is a stronghold.
- ➤ Doubt is a stronghold.
- ➤ Sin or living in sin is a stronghold.
- ➤ Pride is a stronghold. *(To name a few…)*

God's power is the only thing that can destroy fortresses/strongholds. God has given us the key to destroy these strongholds in this world through the Word of God, Prayer, Praise and Intercession.

Believe me when I say that "I've always been taught that you have to believe in something or you'll fall for anything." There's no shame in my game; I believe in (**Ibi**) Santa Claus; (**Ibi**) the Tooth Fairy (got a visit, 25cents from him once); (**Ibi**) Mickey Mouse (was an Official Member of the Club in the 50s); and, (**Ibi**) the Easter Bunny (I was once in the Easter Parade). Also, (**Ibi**) Keeping Hope Alive, Equal Rights, Civil Rights, Human Rights and Social Justice. (**Ibi**) Climate Change and I also believe in Heaven and Hell, the Lake of Fire, and the Power of Prayer. Not to forget that (**Ibi**) Divine intervention (my marriage), the Holy Trinity (Father, Son and Holy Ghost); and I believe that as a Believer, we must continue to Trust God, Grow in Grace, and be led by the Holy Spirit. Know that it's not about believing me or in me; it's about believing in who's within me… JESUS! I truly believe this. What about you? What do you believe?

When we accept God's great love gift (Jesus), we owe Him a wonderful walk of service; and the only way we can even begin to make a token payment is by serving the people His Son (Jesus) died for - you, me and all humanity. Our debt to God must be a love debt, and that is just our reasonable service (Romans 12:1, KJV). Yes, this debt we owe is for God's love (John 3:16, KJV); and although we will never be able to repay that debt, we can work at it while we are in the Kingdom and on this tedious journey (Heaven Bound).

Think about all the benefits we have because of Christ: divine truth, love, grace, peace, wisdom, knowledge, tenderness, kindness, strength, joy, goodness and mercy. How much do we think we owe for all of those things? I believe we must/should pay Him because of all the miraculous things He has done for us, to us and through us. We can begin to pay God by serving Him (1 Samuel 12:24, KJV). Who's ready to get their Serve On? Who's ready to repay?

What if our hearing and reading the word is not enough? What if hearing the preacher preach or the teacher teach isn't enough? What if Bible Study, Sunday School or Prayer Meetings isn't enough? Then what is??? Seriously, take a look around you; c'mon, open your eyes and observe your surroundings, just observe? We are living in an ungodly world. This sinful world is vividly displaying lies, hatred, injustice, deceitfulness, lust and so on... Sadly, it's appalling. Do we, or should we accept these things that's going on in the world? 1 John 2:15-16, KJV tells us to "Love not the world, neither the things that are in the world..." So, what is there left to do??? Where are we now? Where do we go from here? I know I'm preaching to the choir. My Lord! I'd really love to be enlightened. (Matthew 22:37-39, KJV). To God be the Glory!!!

Sometimes in life we feel hopeless, like our living is in vain. We're so heavenly bound that we're no earthly good. We've given Satan a short ride and now he's trying to take the wheel. Like Peter (Matthew 14:28, KJV) we've taken our eyes of the Prize (Jesus) and we're sinking fast... I didn't understand then, but Momma said that'll be days like this. Thank God for Mom and the Holy Spirit. We've all strayed off the path; and now being obedient, the Holy Spirit has guided us back onto the paths of righteousness. Let's continue to be led and stay on the Narrow Path because "narrow is the gate" (Matthew 7:13-14, KJV). Praise God, I'm on it! Who's out there with me?

It's in our nature that we run from any harm, scary situations, and problems and so on... It seems we're always running away leaving a bad situation. We sometimes run from the truth; we run from reality, we run from certain religious groups (no offense), and from our personal calling - in the service of God (some of us). That's why being born again; becoming a New Creature is important, because it changes our carnal nature; thus, we are now Changed in the likeness of Jesus (2 Corinthians 5:17, KJV). Now, we don't run from atheists, unbelievers, or any religious denominations - we run to them. We want to tell them and everyone to "Come See A Man" (John 4:29, KJV). We become a living witness of/about Jesus. ♪♪"I Said I Wasn't Gonna Tell Nobody But I..." So, it's not about us or our carnal nature, we're changed; now, it's about Jesus. Now run and tell that! Go ahead, run on in Jesus Name and tell/bless someone. I'm putting my Nikes on now...

Hebrews 10:24-25, KJV tells us as Believers to assemble encouraging one another. But our faith should go beyond just church attendance. D.C. pastor Mark Batterson, once said "A church that stays within its four walls is not a church at all." Agree to disagree... No, the Church is not a building, it's us - the body of Christ. Hence, it is important that we (our ministry) be a Missional Church of assembled believers that's engaged in the community, economic development, social justice, equality, and have a collaboration with other church assemblies, as Christ will be with us (Matthew 18:20, KJV). God has sent the Church on mission. "As the Father has sent me," Jesus said, "even so I am sending you" (John 20:21 NIV). Christ's mission of His disciples is clear and divine. Are you (The Church) (Your ministry) restricted by four walls?

The God of yesterday, today and tomorrow is still being God; And He keeps on being God; doing what He does unchangingly. What are we doing? Are we Studying to show ourselves approved…Growing in Grace and Knowledge…Pressing Towards the Mark… Letting our lights shine… Putting on the Whole Armor of God… Being a Soldier in the Army… Praying… Visiting… Clothing… Feeding… Worshipping and Praising… Leaning on… Being Filled and Being Led… Not Forsaking the Assembly… and Surrendering All??? I am a witness that: ♪♪"He Just Keeps On Being God – no matter what." Now, I know what I need to do… Family, you're on your own.

Question, is there a Heaven and a Hell? In John 14:3 KJV, Jesus said: "And if I go and prepare a Place for you, I will come again, and receive you unto myself; that where I am, there ye may be also." and in Luke 23:43 KJV, Jesus told one of those crucified with Him "And Jesus said unto him, Verily I say unto thee, today shalt thou be with me In Paradise (Heaven)." Now, if we follow Christ, and He's preparing this Place for us – whereas, we can be with Him (in Paradise); then are we preparing ourselves to go where He is, to be with Him and not go the opposite direction (Hell)? So, what must I/We do to be with Him, after our earthly departure? A serious question and a serious conversation… As I evaluate myself, where I am now and who I am in Him, I'm humbled to say that I'm preparing for a Place prepared for me by Jesus and I'm following Christ to be with Him in Paradise. So, ♪♪"When You Hear Of My Home Going... Don't Worry About Me."

In the constant news cycles, there are international gas explosions, hurricanes, tropical storms, earth quakes, mudslides, and/or wild fires and they all are tragic for many…: Some family has lost their loved one(s); some families have lost their home; and some have lost so much more. As we continue to pray for all families affected, Ephesians 6:10, KJV tells us to: "be strong in the Lord…" and Joshua 1:9, KJV says for us to "Be strong and courageous." Family, we must be encouraged for ourselves and especially for those families going through these devastations. God is still in control... Yes, and God will make it alright; but, we got to stay strong; Pray, and Be Strong for ourselves and Be Strong for those families who have lost loved ones, who have lost their homes, and those who just need our prayers and support. At times, it's impossible to see; But God is going to work it out, if only we continue to believe. Remember this one thing, while you're/we're going through; if God delivered Daniel, Shadrach, Meshach, and Abed-Nego, He'll do the same for me/you/us! He'll do the same for all who have been affected by any local, national or international travesty! We must hold on, because trouble don't last always...These trials we're going through are just a test, but they are just a test of our faith. Hence, Stand Strong; yes, ♪♫"STAND." Pray and Stand for those victims of these past and recent calamities. Pray and Stand on God's Word. Let each one of us, ♪♫"Be Encouraged" and "Stay Strong in the Lord, and in the power of His Might." In obedience to the word, pray and stand, in Jesus' name. Hallelujah!

Can any of us name our price for a heavenly ticket to paradise; myself, I don't want to stay here (this dark world) anymore (I'm just a Pilgrim); I've looked high and low - I've searched from shore, to shore, to shore; If there's a short cut I'd have found it, but there is no easy way around it... ♪♫"Light of the world, shine on me, Love is the answer...Shine on us all, set us free, Love is the answer." Yes, ♪♫"Love is the Answer" (England Dan & John Ford Coley, 1979). Jesus is love; He's the light of the world, and our ticket. Someone said ♪♫"You must come in at the Door" (Rev. Timothy Wright, 2007). Without your Ticket (Jesus) – you cannot enter. Do you have your Ticket to paradise? Do you have Jesus?

Every day, in some form or fashion, each of us is threaten and is witnesses to our own personal trials and tribulations; thus, our faith is rightfully challenged. Even during these surreal times, we are witnessing unprecedented calamities, devastation and despair; ecological and natural disasters, storms, hurricanes, tornadoes, flooding, tsunamis, massive earthquakes, massive wild fires, mass shootings, climate change, flu pandemic, diseases, and famine, with millions globally left homeless. There's human suffering, terrorist threats, wars and rumors of wars. Society has become so lawless and immoral; as the world internationally is spinning in chaos. Yes, these are dire times.

As believers, we are stirred to pray. Scripture tells us, we must watch and pray, and pray without ceasing. Is someone saying: ♪♫"Get right church and let's go home...?" Okay, let's get right, but let us pray in the process. Let's wake up and rejoice, for our redemption draws nigh. If we lose hope, we lose faith. When we lose our faith, we can accidentally or easily "lose" our salvation. In this new world paradigm; and these surreal times we're living in, we can't afford to lose or let go of our Faith. No Way! ♪♫"My faith looks up to Thee, Thou Lamb of Calvary, Savior Divine..." He that hath an ear let him hear what the Spirit saith to the churches... Please read: (Revelations 2:17, KJV) & (Matthew 11:15, KJV); and remember, God is still in control.

God is always at work in our lives. Are there any witnesses? He takes our situations and our circumstances and uses them for our good and His Glory - even though we might not see it at the time. God is constantly wanting and asking us all to draw closer to Him, to depend on Him, to trust Him and allow Him to ♪♫"Keep on Being God, No Matter What..." God reminds us that He is present; ♪♫"He's Just a Prayer Away..." So, sometime during your day or even within any hour of the day, stop, and ♪♫"Have A Little Talk with Jesus." I just know that'll be a wonderful conversation.

Many of us, if not most of us, want to be of service to God, in some form or fashion. We have the faith and we want to work out our soul salvation. Our spiritual health is vibrant and well; but, as Prayer Warriors and Soldiers in the Army of the Lord, we need to be physically healthy – to go where He sends us and run this race. Health is important to travel visiting the sick, shut-ins and incarcerated and to visit towards feeding the hungry. Let's uplift each other in prayer that God would strengthen us physically and spiritually as we stand in need; so, that He can use us. He wants to send us out into the vineyards. Who wants to be used?

When everything is going great, we're saying how good God is. When situations and hardships come against us, we don't hear Gods praises as much. Nevertheless, we know God is present. It's easy to praise God in the light, but we must learn to praise Him in the darkness as well (In season and Out of season). Let's stand on His word during favorable situations and in unfavorable situations. What if we knew that every test and every failure was for our good and God's Glory? Did we know all of (our) those trials and tests were necessary to make us who we are today; and, who we'll we be tomorrow? "And we know that all things work together for good to those who love God, to those who are the called according to His purpose" (Romans 8:28, KJV). Just thinking about it makes me want to get my praise on!

When things are not working as we would expect them, take it as God's subtle way of teaching us to grow (Grow in His Grace and Knowledge). The process may be difficult but it will surely bring the best out of us. Gospel Artist, Vanessa Bell Armstrong reminded me that ♪♫"You (God) Brings Out The Best In Me." And, I'm here as a witness to share with all that He's surely brought out the best in me… what about you? You know God said don't look around because you'll be impressed. Don't look down because you'll be depressed; just look UP - to ME - all the time and you'll be blessed. Yes, you'll be blessed beyond measure… ♪♫"My faith Looks Up to Thee, Thou Lamb of Calvary, Savior divine." Hallelujah!

The Time between our birth and the day the Lord calls us home, that Time is essential to our Salvation. It is during that Time, (that between space), one could ask: "What did we do with it (during it)?" Did we Serve Pray, Trust, Study, Grow, and Follow Christ? This world is not our home we're just Pilgrims traveling thru… During this Time, what are we doing? Are we preparing to be with the Lord? Someone said: ♪♫ "I'm Sending Up My Timbers" ♪♫"I'm Getting Ready" ♪♫"Heaven On My Mind" ♪♫"He's Preparing Me" and, the late Rev. James Cleveland said: ♪♫"I Won't To Be Ready, Any Hour He Spread the Clouds" Others have said, ♪♫"I Want To Be Ready When Jesus Come" ♪♫"It's Time To Get Right With God and Do It Now" and my 1959 Caravans favorite: ♪♫"We're Crossing Over." Heaven is a Prepared Place for Prepared People. Let each of us personally prepare ourselves to be with the Holy Trinity.

Heaven bound… Hallelujah! ♪♪ "I'm Bound For Mt. Zion (Way Out On a Hill)" (The Angelic Gospel Singers, 1975).

We as believers know that none but the RIGHTEOUS shall see God. Not the Religious but the Righteous. 1 John 2:29, KJV says: "If ye know that He isR, ye know that every one that doeth righteousness is born of Him." Have we ever been hungry and Jesus didn't feed us?

Have we ever really needed Him when He didn't need us? Has He ever turned His back on us - when we needed Him to see us through? Have we ever seen someone that was down and out, and Jesus just didn't care about. I don't know about you; but, I've never seen, the Righteous forsaken, or his seed, begging for bread. For it's no secret what our God can do; if He blesses our neighbor, He'll surely bless us too. If we allow Him, He'll dry away all our tears and take away all of our fears. If we just take one step, He'll take two. Oh, it's amazing what the Lord will do. So amazing! No, I've never seen the righteous forsaken, or his seed out begging for bread" (Donald Lawrence & The Tri-City Singers). We (you and I) may be down today, but help is on the way. Yes, dark clouds may dim our sky, but don't worry, He'll answer us by and by. If He's blessed us once He'll bless us twice, and I've personally been living on His blessings all of my life. No, ♪♪ "I've never seen the Righteous forsaken or his seed begging for bread" (The O'Neal Twins, 1985).

Some of us may or may not know that there is a battle between the Flesh and Spirit and we are either Victors or Victims. Ephesians 6:12 (KJV) reminds us: "For we wrestle not against flesh and blood…" Our mind is the battleground that the enemy uses in his attempts to defeat us - daily. Romans 12:2 (KJV) tell us that the key to victory over the flesh is to be transformed by a renewing of the mind. Afterwards, daily victory is achieved by knowing, believing and understanding the battles that we are enduring. Just like Paul, "daily, I battle between the flesh and the Spirit; I hate what I do, and do not accomplish what I want to do." Again, to fight this spiritual battle we must "be transformed by the renewing of our mind" (Ephesians 4:23 KJV). We must Empower ourselves with God's Word as our foundation and keep our minds stayed on Him. The Holy Spirit within us can renew us. If we walk upright, if we hold our peace; and let the Lord fight our battles, we know that the victory shall be ours. Yes, ♪♪ "Victory Shall Be Mine." The Spirit Wins and I am a Victor, Hallelujah!

We all have dreams, fantasies, wishes and desires. I would like to take this time to focus on DISIRE. Yes, I have Desires. I DESIRE to be a vessel for the Lord. An Instrument, a Tool that God can use, for His Glory. My heart's DESIRE is to have a Ministry wholly acceptable to God. To be whom God would have me to be and to do what God would have me to do. I DESIRE a ministry to touch people, as I minister in Jesus' Name. I DESIRE a ministry to teach people the Gospel of Jesus Christ and to go where the Gospel is needed. I DESIRE to be a shining Light in this dark world. In addition, I DESIRE for God to bring out the best in me, through Him and in Him. I have these DESIRES because of scripture: "Trust in the LORD and do good; Delight yourself in the LORD and He will give you the DESIRES of your heart. Commit thy way unto the Lord; trust also in him; and he shall bring it to pass" (Psalm 37:5 KJV). ♫♪"My Desire" (Yolanda Adams).

Have any of us ever had a 2:00 a.m. or 3:00 a.m. O'Dark Thirty moment? Personally, I've had a few. I assume some, if not many of yawl may have also had a few. If you're not sure what it is, take a second to think about it. In the very, early hours of the morning, The Lord (Holy Spirit) wakes you up and speaks to you; He wakes us up and we listen. Sometimes it make be to give us a vision. And, it might not always be a joyful conversation. Sometimes, being corrected can be difficult. However, to realize that the Lord chooses to awaken us, correct, instruct and discipline us, when He could have revoked our privilege all together, should make us smile and say thank you Lord. So, when the Holy Spirit wakens you, be obedient, be alert, and prepare yourself for counsel.

Recently, I was reading Psalm 119 verses 97-108 KJV, when immediately I recognized, with the help of the Holy Spirit, that maybe I wasn't where I needed to be. I felt hungry for understanding, and I had a thirst for knowledge and wisdom (Proverbs 3:13-20, KJV). Then the Holy Spirit enlightened me saying: This is why you read and study God's Word towards growing close to Him. You are no longer under the Law, but under Grace" (Romans 6:14, 15 KJV). I now realize that our practice is in doing; seeing our faults manifest, as we continue towards reading and studying the word. Because we are not satisfied in our spiritual growth, we must also understand and remember that none of us are where we want to be or should be in the Lord (God's Word). It's a process, a way of life, as we "Grow in Grace and in the Knowledge of our Lord and Savior Jesus the Christ" (2 Peter 3:18 KJV). Thank You Holy Spirit!

Let's Trust Him! Little trials without God will break us. Big trials with God will make us great. May we always Trust and find strength in God's love and faithfulness. Trusting God won't make the mountain smaller but it will make climbing it easier. I pray that all who reads this Spiritual Message will be able to Trust God and that we continue to climb all our mountains, big or little. Have We've all said at one time or another that we want God to use us Are we ready for God to use us? Rhetorically; ask yourselves, Am I ready to be used? Am I where He wants me to be - to be used? Ephesians 6:10 KJV says: "Be strong in the Lord and in the power of His might." Am I strong enough? If you are ready for God to use you in any manner, ask Him. "Master, Can You Use Me?" We may consider ourselves too inadequate, too prone to failure, or just too sinful to serve an almighty, all powerful, and Holy God. Isaiah 6:5 (KJV) said, "Woe is me" when he was confronted with the presence of the Lord, yet he declared, "Here am I, send me." It's too easy for us to sit back and think that God cannot use us because we don't have certain abilities or opportunities that others have. In spite of our sin, God wants to use us and He equips us to be fit for (the Master's) His service. If we Believed the word of God; we should also believe in the Power of God; and, we'll realized our responsibility before God. Now, rhetorically ask yourselves again: ♪♫"Master, Can You Use Me?" and Lord, "Here Am I, Send Me" (Isaiah 6:8, NIV)!

It's easy to blame God and others for all our problems; because if we blame others, we don't have to take any personal responsibility. Yes, we get hurt; we sure do, but we are still responsible for what we do with that hurt. We do not have to go through the pain of dealing with our part in it all, but we also don't heal! I'm an advent supporter of Obamacare, Single-payer health care system and anyone who has a pre-existing condition and need healing. Here's a reminder: ♪♫"There Is a Balm in Gilead" Nevertheless, we have to stop blaming God for the messes we put ourselves in at times. We made those poor choices, no one else did. Okay, some of us have made very bad decisions; we chose to go left when God (Holy Spirit) said to go right. We want to blame God. What we all need to do is; instead of blaming God, ask Him for forgiveness and guidance. This will definitely make our lives better. Besides, God doesn't play the "blame game" and we shouldn't either. My pre-existing condition was sin; now, I am redeemed. Hallelujah!

We all have plan and/or have planned. All of us know that God has a plan; and, we are a part of His plan whether we know it or not; whether we like it or not; whether we accept it or not, we're still a part of it. Personally, do you know His plan for you? If the answer is no, then find out! If the answer is yes, Hallelujah! Okay, we've established that God has a plan, now we ask ourselves: are we (you and I) where God want us to be in Christ Jesus? Are we (you and I) satisfied with where we are in Christ Jesus? For one thing, I do not want to be playing church anymore. My (our) salvation is a serious matter. Some of us, if not most of us have ♪♫ "Come thus far by faith, leaning on the Lord, Trusting in His Holy Word..." We know who we are (in Christ) and whose we are (Christs'); and we (you and I) will trust in the Lord until we die... C'mon yawl, Trust Him!

If it had not been for the Lord on my side - Where would I be? Fortunately, if the Lord hadn't reached waaaay down to pick me up out of the miry clay; (He brought me up out of the pit of destruction...) I wouldn't be (**IWB**) an Apostle, a Prophet, an Evangelists, a Pastor or a Teacher; (**IWB**) a Member of the Body of Christ, a Disciple of Christ, a Child of the King, or a Soldier in the Army of the Lord; (**IWB**) a Pray Warrior, (**IWB**) on the Prayer Line, attend Bible Study, or Church/Sunday School; (**IWB**) Running for Jesus; and, (**IWB**) Worshipping or Praising His Name. ♪♫"If it had not been for the Lord on our side, where would we be" (Psalm 118:6, KJV)? Myself, I wouldn't be writing these Spiritual Messages; and, you probably wouldn't be reading them. Amen.

For the purpose of growing in Grace, don't ever run ahead of God. We follow Him! ♪♫"Where He Leads Me I will Follow," (Luke 9:57, KJV). Let Him direct (order) your steps. He has His plans and He has His time. God's clock is never early nor late, is it always on time. Sometimes in life we tend to run so fast we don't even notice God running with us. We only notice Him when we trip and fall; yet, He stops and carries us. When we encounter problems in life, we should never ask God to take them away. Ask Him for strength to engage them. Ask Him to show His purpose. Ask Him ways how to live each day searching His purpose for us. Ask Him; Lord, "Order My Steps?" C'mon, try Him?

I beseech all in the name of our Lord to grow in grace and knowledge of Him. It is important that we grow in our relationship with Jesus Christ. Hence, it is somewhat of importance because we are who we are because of our past. Yes, we all have a past, whether good or bad, memorable or undesirable; but our past is just the past. We all know that we shouldn't dwell in the past because we're pressing forward towards the Mark… **HISTORY** (Not worldly) is important to each of us. Not like our past, **HISTORY** is of the utmost importance concerning our salvation. It is necessary because it concerns our historical relationship with the Trinity. It's essential to have and make **HISTORY** with the Father, the Son, and the Holy Spirit. Even Peter at the Pearly Gates would agree… Our **HISTORY** (still being written) is the measure that solidifies our future of Salvation, our eternal Life and our names written in the Book of Life. No, it's not our past we should dwell on, but our **HISTORY**. Our **HISTORY** with the Trinity will ensure our future of Eternal Life. We can let go of the past, make **HISTORY** and secure our future. (Psalm 37:5, KJV) I'm just sayin' - Now, what are we waiting for?

Some of yawl just might be familiar with these lyrics: ♪♫"If it wasn't for the Lord, where would I be, my life was nothing until He set me free. What a change He made in my life, no more compromising the wrong for the right. He Made The Difference (**HMTD**): He made the difference in my life. I don't talk and walk like I used to, (**HMTD**). I don't live and give like I used to, (**HMTD**). I don't praise & worship for form or fashion like I used to, (**HMTD**). Yes, He made the difference in my life…" Jesus definitely made the difference in my life! Right about now, I'm feeling good…because, "He Made The Difference!" (James Bignon) Hallelujah!

There are a couple of songs that've been deeply on my mind; and I've been spiritually overwhelmed with them. I've been humming and singing them for years. The first one is called: ♪♫"I'm Willing" I'm Willing To Wait on The Lord God Almighty"- by: (The Caravans, 1958). Let us continue to Pray, Trust, Stand and Wait on God. Yes, wait on the Lord. I'm a witness; I can guarantee, that He may not come exactly when you want Him to; but, He will be on time. Are You Willing? Are You Willing to wait on the Lord God Almighty? In season and out of season, WAIT! Because if you wait ♪♫"He'll Be There" (The O'Neal Twins, 1985). I was Willing to Wait, and He came and He was on time…

Who told us we can save ourselves? Humanly, it is impossible to save ourselves but very possible for God. We cannot save ourselves. We can't even save others. We are not called to save others, but merely help them (by the life we live in Christ) to see what God has already done, and continues to do, in their lives. No matter what we might have heard, only the Lord has the power to save. Jesus had to die on the cross because we couldn't save ourselves. We must understand that we can only be saved by trusting in Christ Jesus. "Lord, Save Me" and please, ♪♫"Lord, Save Me From Myself"… Yes, sometimes we're our own worst sinful enemy. No, we can't save ourselves because it only takes just one sin to separate us from God. That one sin distorts our efforts to do good; and the good works we do are not sufficient to save us. All sin is against God. God is against all sin. It's only by God's grace we have been saved. Are You in God's Grace? Do You feel Saved? For by grace we have been saved through faith, and this is not our own doing; it is the gift of God not the result of works, so that none of us may boast (Ephesians 2:8-9, ESV). Our soul (yours & mine), though it can be lost, it can also be saved; but definitely, not by us alone. Jesus Saves! ♪♫"To The Utmost Jesus Saves!"

Biblically, we've read: "Owe no man anything, but to love one another" (Romans 13:8, KJV)." No, it is not referring to owing someone money; it means we are not to owe even one person anything when it comes to divine love and the things of God. Jesus said, "By this shall all men know that ye are my disciples, if ye have love one to another (John 13:35, KJV)." When we meet people who need the love, the hope, the faith, the goodness, the tenderness, the humility and the grace of God, we must serve them those things. Because of Jesus' great sacrifice, we are debtors to lost souls; and we owe them. Paul said, "I am debtor both to the Greeks, and to the Barbarians; both to the wise, and to the unwise (Romans 1:14, KJV)." As servants of God, we are debtors to all human beings. Pay your debt.

Anyone in a storm? We do not always understand the cause of the storms but they come into all of our lives. None of us is immune from them and when they hit - they are unexpected, they are scary and they point to a God greater than ourselves. Our storms are whatever we are facing today… Perhaps it's a health issue, financial issue, death of a loved one, a job loss, a difficult boss, an unsupportive family member, friend, church, or a wayward child or wayward spouse. Maybe you are exhausted with unanswered prayers and you are scared, lonely, heartbroken, or depressed. Just remember - The Lord is our good shepherd and He never leaves our side. He walks with us through the valleys. He restores our soul when we are weary. He leads us to the path of righteousness when we have lost our way. He gives us courage when we are scared and He comforts us when we are hurting. Our God can be trusted! He sees and knows all the details of our private storms. He will take care of us. He loves us so. May we not be conceived – but rather allow our storms to bring us humbly to the throne of Jesus to seek guidance (Holy Spirit) and help us in our days of trouble. Glory!

I've always heard that time is of the essence; Time is valuable; Time is now; Time flies; Time heals all wounds; Time is moving; Time is money; Time brings all thoughts to past; Lost time is never found again; and, Quiet time…(Ecclesiastes 3:1-8, KJV). Okay, some of us have time for everything: Facebook, texting, the gym, partying, plotting, scheming, grooming, and gossiping to name a few. We as believers have to make time for God, during our so called busy schedules. Investing over time in God (His Word) has the greatest rate of returns. Our spiritual growth is not just reading (scripturally), but lived. Spending quiet time with God is simple, not mysterious. It's also said that time is precious; and there's only one thing more precious than our time and that's who we spend it on or with. Do we have time for God? If the answer is yes, how much is allocated to Him? Do we spend Time with Him? Time is free, but it's priceless. We can't own it, but we can use it. We can't keep it, but we can borrow it; and once we lose it, we can never get it back. Is Time On Our Side? Umm…Give Him yours!

The essence of Worship is Heartfelt, Hope-filled Joy in God. When we truly Worship, We Get Joy, God Gets Praise (John 4:23, KJV). "God is a Spirit: and they that worship him must worship him in spirit and in truth" (John 4:24, KJV). The closer we get to the Lord, the better we will get to know Him. Please, read the following translations of Corinthians 3:18; KJV, ESV, and NLT? The Holy Spirit transforms us from the inside out. None of us can't be like Christ if we're not reflecting Christ, and we can't reflect Christ if we don't first behold Him. ♪♫"Now Behold the Lamb" It's Not About Me! It's About Jesus! I'm ready to WORSHIP! I was born to WORSHIP! Were You?

It's our carnal nature to have faith. No one can live a single day without exercising faith. Everyone places his or her faith in something or someone. Yes, everybody has some type of faith and we have faith in many different things. The Moslem puts his faith in the Koran and in Mohammed. The humanist put his faith in himself. A religious person puts his faith in his own good works; whereas, a RIGHTEOUS person puts his faith in God. Scriptures tell us we're to personally put our faith and trust in Jesus. "Neither is there Salvation in any other: for there is none other name under heaven given among men, whereby we must be saved" (Acts 4:12, KJV). Yet, some still think that as long as they are sincere about what they believe then that faith will be good enough. Paul tells us "for I know whom I have believed and am persuaded that He is able to keep what I have committed to Him until that Day (2 Timothy 1:12, KJV). Faith is the affirmative response to God's Will and Word. Man encompasses faith when He takes God at His Word. We don't need to see something to believe it. Faith is the acceptance of something simply because God has said it. In John 20:29 KJV, Jesus said,

"… blessed are they that have not seen, and yet have believed." Yes, everyone has faith and inevitably, the storms of life will blow (where mighty billows roll). So, all of us need an anchor that will hold. That anchor is our faith. The question is where is my faith anchored? Please, Anchor it to Christ! ♪♪"My Soul Is Anchored In The Lord"

I found myself nostalgically reminiscing of my faith-walk and path to salvation; and what came to mind was that, I don't think anyone of us have been holy and/or saved all of our lives – that we tell… Only some of us pretend and act as if we've always lived on the straight and narrow… Never went to a Bar or danced at the Club… Never drank alcohol, sniffed glue, or did any type of drugs... Never smoked Marijuana, cigarettes, or gotten high... Remembering how we'd find a way to sneak into the drive-ins, movie theatres, into house parties or other facilities, without paying. How we'd climb over the fence, snuck or went around the back way to get in somewhere without permission. We thought we were 'slick-as-rick' and we knew it. There wasn't a door that could be shut or locked to keep us out. There's no way we were going to pay the entry or entrance fee. Not knowing or realizing then that the entry/entrance fee for our salvation had already been paid! Yes, Jesus paid it all…

In John 10:9 (KJV), Jesus said: "I am the door: by me if any man enter in, he shall be saved" Well, for-your-information (F.Y.I.) - remember, ♪♪"You Must Come In At The Door" (Rev. Timothy Wright): "God's got a way (that we can't go over), God's got a way (that we can't go under), God's got a way (that we can't go around); You/Me/We Must Come in at the Door. There's no other way but, by Jesus. He's The Way in. There's no other way into the Kingdom of God. Sorry, No other way. We can't sneak in and we can't pay. There's no entry fee accepted or needed, because Salvation is Free, Hallelujah!!! There's no other way… but, by Jesus. He's The Way! Hallelujah!!!

So, it's not just me…We've all gone through the storm and the rain; the hurt, and the pain (some still). We've continuously been entangled in ongoing trials and tribulation. And because of Christ, we didn't give up. No matter how harsh life gets; no matter how difficult, every brother every sister out here ♪♪"Don't Give Up!" (Island Inspirational All Stars, 1995) Please, enjoy these inspirational lyrics?

> ♪♪ "I know the day is dim chances may be slime, hold on to what you believe.
> I know it hurts inside sometimes you sit and cry,
> but you gotta hold on to what you believe.
> Trouble only last for a while, but joy is gonna come with the morning light.
> And to every life some rain must fall, but trials they come to make us strong….

Don't Give Up!"♪ Yes Lord, we've all gone through the storm and the rain; the hurt, and the pain (some of us are still going through as we're reading…). And because of Christ, we didn't give up. No matter how hard it is/gets (life); no matter how rough, every brother every sister out here, be strong… ♪♫"Don't Give Up!"

I assume we all have in our possession God's Word (The Bible) with many of man's translations; which is our choice or preference to purchase at local book stores. But there's one book that we will not find at any bookstore. 'The Book of Life' This Book records all who will receive God's gift of eternal life. When God writes our name down in the Book of Life, there's no one that can take it out but YOU/ME/US. As long as we live according to the Will of God *(not our will but Thy Will Be Done)* our name will remain in the Book of Life. Luke 10:20, KJV reminds us to "rejoice because our names are written in heaven." The Book that belongs to Jesus Christ is called the "Lamb's Book of Life" Revelation 21:27, KJV). To have one's name written in this book means that one is considered of Christ and is righteous before God and will inherit eternal life provided he or she remains faithful to the end (Revelation 3:5, KJV). To have one's name blotted out of this book signifies a fate of eternal death (Revelation 20:15, KJV).

Some bible Scholars agree to disagree that The Book of Life and the Lamb's Book of Life are one and the same. Hint they both are Salvation related; the Bible doesn't contradict. Read the Scriptures for yourself… Pray and ask God to enlighten you. Note, all that matters is it is us alone that has control over whether we get our name written in Heaven or not. No man can put our name in this Book (Lamb's) and no man can take it out. When God Opens 'The Book of Life' will Your Name be written there? Or, will it be Blotted Out? So, those of us who are true Born Again Believers in Christ, led by His Holy Spirit, names are written in the 'Lamb's Book of Life' Along with the Holy Spirit, yawl decide, if both Books are the same. Rhetorically, Where's Your Name Written? Glory!!! "Hallelujah! "Praise God from whom all blessings flow…

In another message, I shared that we were either a Sheep or a Goat. Some might say that our Salvation and Eternal Life depends ultimately not on what we do; or fail to do, but on what we are – Sheep (passive, easily led) or Goats (non-passive, headstrong). Isaiah 53:6 (KJV) reminds us that "Like Sheep, we all have gone astray – doing our own thing" (Romans 3:23, KJV: "for all have sinned…") Matthew 10:16, ESV reminds us that He (Jesus) is the Son of man who sends us out like Sheep among wolves. And, John 10:27, ESV asks us if we know our Shepherd's Voice, when He calls us; and do we Follow Jesus, as Sheep follow the "Good Shepherd" (John 10:11, 14, KJV). Lastly, Psalm 33 KJV says: "The Lord is My Shepherd." In John 5:22 KJV, God has given the Son (Jesus) the authority to judge; Matthew 25:31-33 KJV says: "When the Son of Man comes in His glory, and all the angels with Him, He will sit on his glorious throne. All the nations will be gathered before Him, and He will separate the people one from another, as a shepherd separates the sheep from the goats. He will put the sheep on His <u>right</u> and the goats on His <u>left</u>. It is inevitable that we will be judged... so, rhetorically; ask ourselves, "are we a Sheep or a Goat?" Our Salvation depends on being on the Left or Right of Christ. Umm...

We are reminded "To everything there is a season, and a time to every purpose under the heaven..." (Ecclesiastes 3:1, KJV) Yes, the Book of Ecclesiastes provides us instruction on how we're to live meaningfully, purposefully and joyfully within the theocratic arrangement of our time (Season); primarily by placing God at the center of one's life, work and activities, by contentedly accepting one's divinely appointed lot in life, and by reverently trusting in and obeying the Creator, God. We all have seasons. Wherever you are in your season, understand it will pass. We must respect and hold on to this time because God planned us to be there for His purpose (Glory) and our good. Remember, we are a part of God's Plan, whether we know it or not, whether we accept it or not. God loves us! During your season lean on Him. Continue praising Him in season and out of season. ♪♪"Glory Hallelujah!" In the Book of Ecclesiastes 3:1-8 (KJV), it says:

1. To everything there is a season, and a time to every purpose under the heaven:
2. A time to be born, and a time to die; a time to plant, and a time to pluck up that which is planted;
3. A time to kill, and a time to heal; a time to break down, and a time to build up;
4. A time to weep, and a time to laugh; a time to mourn, and a time to dance;
5. A time to cast away stones, and a time to gather stones together; a time to embrace, and a time to refrain from embracing;
6. A time to get, and a time to lose; a time to keep, and a time to cast away;
7. A time to rend, and a time to sew; a time to keep silence, and a time to speak;
8. A time to love, and a time to hate; a time of war, and a time of peace.

Now is our time, our season; besides, we have very little time left because "We must work the works of Him that sent us, while it is day: the night cometh, when no man can work (John 9:4, KJV).

While writing these messages, you might've noticed that they've been inundated with supporting scriptures. Being obedient, the Holy Spirit led me to incorporate more scriptures. God's Word is important to all of us; if we're on the path to becoming righteous and attaining salvation. The psalmist wrote, "Your word is a lamp to my feet and a light to my path" (Psalm 119:105, KJV). In these messages, you might've also noticed that God has spoken (*Let the Church Say Amen*), and is still speaking to us. Apostle Paul says in 2 Timothy 3:16-17, KJV:

"All Scripture is given by inspiration of God, and is profitable for doctrine, for reproof, for correction, for instruction in righteousness..." Yes, God's Word (Scripture) is sufficient. God's Word is Truth which enunciates the Person of Truth, Jesus Christ. "The sum of Your word is truth" (Psalm 119:160, KJV). Lastly, Isaiah 55:11, KJV tells us God's word will not return void; because He is sovereign in His omniscience, omnipotence, and omnipresence. And as Believers, as Christians, Scripture is also essential to our spiritual growth and maturity; thus, it is life-changing. Is anyone born again? So, please read the scriptures, hear the word, be doers and live the word and don't just be hearers only (James 1:22, KJV); "the word of God for the people of God."

Here's some "Food For Thought," overlooking the carbs, is it safe to say - most of us love bread. If we didn't have meat what would we eat? Bread! Bread is common to every person; it is a staple of life. Just a piece of Bread is what most third world countries are sadly without. Some of us or many of us may or may not know it, but we are spiritually hungry and we're looking for what will satisfy the ache (hunger pains) in our souls. Jesus is what satisfies the hungry soul. He is the Bread of Life. He is our sufficiency; He is what hungry souls are longing for. Jesus cares for us; He can, and He will provide for us. He and only He can definitely satisfy our hunger. Family, let us break Bread (Study the Word) together and forget about Carbohydrates. Right about now, I'd love to have some Manna from Heaven. Starving for it! Who's Hunger? Scriptures reminds us that Jesus fed 5000+ who were gathered on the shore of Galilee. Personally, "I have not seen the righteous forsaken, nor his seed begging bread." (Psalm 37:25, KJV) He can feed You/Me/Us! Is anyone hungry? Anyone want some Bread/ Manna?

Some may think otherwise, but we are not our own; we were bought at a high price. Because of John 3:16 (KJV), what should we render to God? We should therefore honor God with our body (1 Corinthians 6:19-20, KJV). Our body is (should be) a place dedicated to worship. Our body includes a divine presence within it. Our body is a place reserved for a highly valued function. We should consider our body as an important edifice. It is not only the foundation on which our good health and well-being is based, but we (each of us) individually are the caretakers of our own body and our soul. As Caretakers of our body, as a believer in Jesus Christ, we must allow God to take up permanent residence in our body "He lives with you and will be in you" (John 14:17, KJV). We have the third person of the Trinity, the Holy Spirit living in us. After accepting Christ as our personal Savior, the Holy Spirit comes to live within us (in us) spiritually. Colossians 1:27, KJV says that we as believers are indwelt... The indwelling of the Holy Spirit (our inner sanctum) is the inner sanctum of God, as we become sanctified and forgiven by the blood of Jesus (Ephesians 1:7, KJV). Lastly, as Caretakers of our body, as a follower and believer in Jesus, we became the habitation of the Holy Spirit of

God. When we accepted Christ as our Savior (Romans 10:9-13, KJV), the Holy Spirit takes up resident, now our body is indwelt spiritually by Christ (Colossians 1:27, KJV) and by God the Father (1 John 4:15, KJV). Is your house (residence) in order, clean, available? Are you open for a tenant (Holy Spirit)? Is your body (Temple) ready and open for service?

I truly believe some of us are not happy with where we are in Christ. No; we're not close enough, we're not in Him as much as we want to be or, should be. Without Christ, we know life is hard. I'm for growing in Christ. I'm working hard in faith to be like Him (Jesus) because Musical Artist Lionel Richie reminds me: "everybody wants me to be what they want me to be" and I only want to be like Jesus - not like Mike! So, I'm not happy or satisfied with where I am in Christ. I want to be closer. I want to be like Him. Do we all? Yawl please excuse me; it's growing time (2 Peter 3:18, KJV), I have my Bible in hand and the Counselor HE SENT - now school's in.

I'm very interested to know if someone can rhetorically explain; how can we act right, do right, live right, talk and walk right, if we're not in the Righteousness of God? The term "righteousness" appears in the Book of Romans more than sixty times. "Righteousness" is the position of being totally acceptable to, and accepted by God. Each of us as Christians and/or Believers became acceptable to God when the sin that stood between us and God was washed away by the blood of Jesus. Thus, "Righteousness" is our standing in the sight of God as believers who are "righteous" and "accepted" in spite of our sins, failures, and shortcomings. Umm, Man's right vs. God's Righteousness? Some, if not only a few of us believe we are right most, if not all of the time.

We must understand that there's our right (what we think, good or bad) and God's Right. It's not debatable; it's God's Way, God's Purpose, God's Will, God's Plan, and God's Right. We as Believers, Christians, Followers, and Children of God have to Get Right with Him in order for Him to use us; for Him to order our steps, for Him to continuously bless us as we stand in need, and for Him to keep us and never leave us nor forsake us. We should never confuse our worldly right, or what we call or think is right to what is Right in the eyes of God. God is always right. No matter how things may look from our human perspective, no matter how confused life seems to be, no matter how uncomfortable we are with the circumstances of our lives, this is a truth we can hold on to: God is always right. It's The Righteousness of God! ♪♪"Get Right Church..." In Romans 1:17, (KJV) Paul tells us: "For therein is the Righteousness of God revealed from faith to faith: as it is written, the just shall live by faith." It's all about our Faith and His Righteousness!

Family, I know that you are fully aware that every day, death knocks on the doors of someone somewhere; taking a family member (Mother, Sister, etc...), like a friend, a child, a 13 year old girl, or a sports Superstar. Although it's unfortunately, death comes naturally or catastrophically. It takes whoever God allows it to take. It affects each of us differently but painfully. Of course we initially feel numb and disoriented; we mourn as we do now in (Detroit), (St. Louis), (Calabasas,

California), (Alabama) and/or other places worldwide. We must pray for the bereaved families that are physically and emotionally affected. In their Bereavement, (state of intense grief), we're all praying for God to comfort them and ease their pain. To ease our pain in this period of sadness, we must cling to God's promises as we work through our grief because He gives us power in our hour of weakness as He increases our strength, (Isaiah 40:29, KJV). Jesus said, "I will not leave you comfortless: I will come to you" (John 14:18 KJV). Let Him? Sadly praying for all who have recently lost someone... "Jesus wept" as I... (John 11:32-35, KJV)

I beseech you, my brothers and sisters in the name of our Lord Jesus Christ. I'm praying that each of you will be spiritually enlightened by this very important spiritual, and teachable message. I'm hoping some, if not most of us make preparation for everything we do. We get ready for work, school, vacation, partying, church, etc... Yes, we are ready for most things; and yes, we want to be ready for whatever "come what may;" such as disasters, emergencies, accidents, etc... Some of us proclaim we're getting ready for Christ's return, for eternal life, when our roll is called up yonder... We say "we want to be ready." Are we? There will be a Second Coming of Jesus Christ. Yes, Jesus is coming back, and when he returns, will He find us awake and alert or sleeping and slumbering? Jesus will return for His Church. He will come to receive those of us who are waiting for Him and are **Ready** to meet Him. (John 14:1-3, KJV) He's coming for those of us who have accepted Him (Jesus) as our Savior and are spirit-led. This is the event that we know as the Rapture. The Bible calls this the blessed hope (Titus 2:13, KJV). No doubt, Jesus is coming again, the question is, Are You Ready? One of my Spiritual mentors, an iconic Gospel Great - the late Rev. James Cleveland (and I), would like not to be an inconvenience but would like share a small synopsis of this song with you:

> ♪♪ "A lot of people playing church nowadays;
> No doubt if we just ask the question how many are saved -
> a whole lot of folks would raise their hands."
> "I'd like to tell yawl something:
> Everybody talking about Heaven - Ain't Going; Everybody singing about Heaven...."
> There's a lot of things I wanna be But I Wanna Be Ready, when He comes!" ♪

As Followers, Believers, and Christians, we should always be mentally, emotionally, and Spiritually ready for any challenge the world brings us, so that we will be ready for Christ's return. I'm praying we'll all be ready. Ready (Luke 12:40, KJV) and (Matthew 24:36-44, KJV). "I Want To Be Ready" Thank You Jesus!!!

Am I grateful? Are We Grateful? Many, if not all of us have issues; especially, health issues.

Yes, some of our issues are more serious than others; probably, life threatening. Regardless of the level and because of who we are (Child of God) and whose we are (Christ'), we are still grateful. We are grateful even when we've endured unimaginable pain and tragedy. One of the most important things we must do when and however we suffer is to give thanks. We thank God during the good times and the bad times. Oh yes, we pray and we leave it at the altar. We have a strong and growing faith that God would heal us physically, emotionally, and spiritually however He pleases and whenever He pleases. We're in God's Hands, all of us; and He blesses each of us accordingly. Don't let our issues and circumstances prolong our blessings. Let us stay in His Favor; being what He would have us to be, to be healthily blessed. ♪♪"Be Grateful" and May God heal each of us in His time however!

I haven't given this (hypocrisy) much thought but, as led by the Holy Spirit, I do believe it's worth discussing. I was browsing through the Old Testament and the Holy Spirit led me to the 2nd Chapter of Isaiah (KJV), where the prophet Isaiah gave the people a warning. It made me think and ask: "Will our hypocritical nature be our downfall?" Webster cites that a Hypocrite is someone who says one thing but does another, a person who is two-faced, who is inconsistent or phony. Hypocrisy can also be defined as "behavior that does not agree with what someone claims to believe or feel." What do you believe and feel? Some, if not most of us believe and fear God, and we are reverent before Him.

A Godly life requires us to make a choice by accepting Christ and to be in God's Will and to follow God's Will; (Romans 12:1–2, KJV). Yes, the Lord has called us as believers to live a (Godly) Holy life (1 Peter 1:16 KJV), but we cannot be Holy without His help and guidance from the Holy Spirit. No, we can't fake it. We must strive away from our hypocritical nature and become the more authentic believer God has created us to be; hence, not heading towards any disastrous downfall. And let our goal in life and the remedy for hypocrisy be that our heavenly Father (and only Him) truly sees what we do, along with our thoughts and our petitions. Not giving leeway to form or fashion, let us also be less concerned for the approval of men and more focused on and satisfied with the approval of God. Amen!!! Please, take time to read Matthew Chapter 6, KJV and NIV. Yield not to Hypocrisy...

We all know there's right and there's wrong, there's good and evil/bad. There's also a heaven and a hell. Most of us want to live right, and avoid hell (Lake of Fire); at least we say we do. We want to walk, talk, and act right; sometimes we struggle, but we do strive for righteousness. Can we do it alone? It's our carnal nature to do our own thing; like to sin and be selfish and do wrong to ourselves and to others.

I believe it's the wrong Trinity of - Me, Myself & I. Some forget that it's not about me/us. Some of us call ourselves loners and that we don't need anyone; and we think and believe we're right most of the time, if not all of the time. I'm reminded opposite of one hip hop artist song, "This is not how we do it." This isn't right. It's not right in the eyes of God. God didn't create us to be alone or to be sinful. He said that He'd never leave us nor forsake us; and that we are His redeemed. So, who's alone and who's right. Better yet, Who Wants to See God? "Blessed are the pure in heart: for they shall see God." (Matthew 5:8, KJV) We must be Pure in heart. As His redeemed, we must be RIGHTeous! If we haven't already, let's begin to live RIGHT; and like one of my spiritual sisters always say: "Live On Purpose!" I'm talking about a purpose of Purity and Righteousness in Christ Jesus. We're not alone, together we can do this. It's us; you, me, and the Trinity. It's the Right thing to do! Now, will yawl please excuse me, I have Company (The Trinity)! It's Praise and Worship Time.

In Romans 7:19-20 ESV, Paul tells us: "For I do not do the good I want to do, but the evil I do not want to do this I keep on doing. Now if I do what I do not want to do, it is no longer I who do it, but it is sin living in me that does it." The principle of sin has possessed itself of all our carnal appetites and passions; and thus, subjects our reason and domineers over our soul. Are we in God's Will? If we are, then our Will is against, or opposed to sin/evil. It is not our Will that leads men astray; but the corrupt passions which oppose and oppress our Will. It's a blessing to know that the Will (ours) is on the side of God and truth. Did you know that our Will has the power to see what is good, and to distinguish between that and evil; to acknowledge its purity and to Will it from conviction. Yes Lord, I thank you, "Thy Will Be Done." God's will for our lives have reason and purpose. (Jeremiah 29:11, KJV) "It is the will of God." I pray we are aligning our Will with God's Will; submitting ourselves to Him, while asking that His way not our way triumphs. We must surrender our Will to God. Before God will begin to reveal His Will to us, we must be committed to doing whatever it is that He desires for us to do. Let us practice to obey what we already know to be God's Will. Remember, our Will is to follow God's Plan, stay in His Will and to trust in it! This is God's will for our life! "It is the will of God." To God be the Glory!

Jesus was the ultimate sacrifice (Sacrificial Lamb of God), John 1:29, NIV. We follow Him, so what have we sacrificed? We say/sing ♪♫"I Surrender All" have we? Again, what have we sacrificed? Remember, "Jesus paid it all. All to Him we owe..." Yes, We Owe! You and I, we live for Him because of the life that we have through Him; and because of His death on the cross; and by God's grace, we owe everything to Him, (Romans 11:36, KJV). No, we are not our own; we were bought at a price; and no, we cannot repay God for what He's done (John 3:16, KJV), but we do have an obligation. Therefore, we as the redeemed are obligated to honor God with our bodies, (1 Corinthians 6:19-20, KJV). Our obligation is to give our bodies as a living sacrifice because again, we live for Christ, (Romans 12:1, KJV)! So, if we are like Christ, if He lives in us, and we are His, then we should be living sacrifices! Are you?

Do we really know what it means to be blessed by God or what a blessing is? Are you blessed? Can you count your blessings? It's crucial that we take a personal inventory of the unmerited blessings of God we have received. God has blessed some of us if not most of us, immeasurably. I pray that each of you truly know and appreciate the blessings you have in Christ? If not, please resolve to have an attitude like Christ. An attitude of Christ is a Blessing! Yes, "Our attitude should be the same as that of Christ Jesus" Philippians 2:5 (NIV). In Genesis 12:2 (ESV), the Lord said to Abraham: "I will make you a great nation, and I will bless you, and make your name great, so that you will be a blessing." So, Yawl be blessed today and while you're being blessed, be a blessing.

We've all heard that "God Can Do Anything But Fail." Has He ever failed you? No, because He's Able... I'm a living witness that He's Able, Able to solve those impossible issues, overwhelming circumstances, and/or problems we constantly endure in our lives (Matthew 19:26 NIV). He's Able only if we yield our will fully to Him and commit to Him in prayer believing that He will solve them in His own perfect way and His perfect time. He's able to do everything He wills ("Thy Will Be Done"). He's Able to Keep Us from Sin (stumbling). He is Able to Supply All Our Needs. Yes, "God is able to do immeasurably more than all we can ever ask or imagine" (Ephesians 3:20-21 NIV). We're not to limit Him; NO, we can't limit God. He's Able to do what He has promised (Luke 1:37 NIV). There is no deficiency in His power - NONE. Simply, the Lord is Able! ... and willing! (Mark 1:41, KJV). Again, Yes God is able - Trust Him... "Let go and Let God." Hallelujah!

Some, many, if not all of us have made Sacrifices of some sort. Have you ever asked yourself, what do I need to do to please God? What is the best that each one of us can do for our God? SACRIFICE! What is God asking us to let go (Sacrifice) or leave behind? What are we hanging on to, that we're so unwilling to sacrifice for God? (Romans 12:1, KJV) What are we grasping so tight that we can't let go of? If God asked you to let it go, would you? Would you make the Sacrifice? Something is competing for our devotion to God. Whatever it is, that's what we have to let go - To Sacrifice!

For some of us, it may be an inappropriate relationship. Maybe it is an addiction to alcohol, drugs or porn. Maybe it's time from our so called busy schedules. Maybe it's our attitude, social media, our love for money; our ambitions, the company we keep, or more... We must give up (Sacrifice) whatever keeps us from following Jesus, trusting our life fully to Him. As with the Disciples back then, Jesus is inviting us today, right now, to (Sacrifice) leave carnal/earthly attachments behind and follow Him. Yes, He's asking us for a great Sacrifice, while offering the Promise of great joy. (Mark 8:34, 35, KJV) When we follow Christ, it's a Sacrifice! (Matthew 16:24-25, KJV) Remember John 3:16 (KJV), God Sacrificed His Son, Jesus Sacrificed His life. What are we sacrificing? What have we sacrificed? God's reward will more than overcome any Sacrifice we have to make or have made. Thank you for sacrificing your precious time to read this lengthy message.

It's inevitable that we are constantly faced with the everyday trials and tribulations of life. There's a lot going on and it's nothing new. Family, please join me in Prayer? "Lord, I praise and thank you for your great love for me. Thank you for delivering me over and over again. Thank you for hearing my cry. Lord, thank you for the sufficiency of your grace (unmerited favor) (Ephesians 1:6, KJV), and your act of mercy (forgiveness). I thank you for Jesus and the "Helper" (John 14:16, KJV). Thank You Lord!" Amen.

So, ♪♪"What Shall I Render, To God. What Shall I Sacrifice, As An Offering?" In Matthew 22:21 ESV, Jesus said, "RENDER to Caesar the things that are Caesar's; and to God the things that are God's." And Romans 13:1, NASB say, "Let every person be in subjection to the governing authorities. For there is no authority except from God and those which exist are established by God." Recently, I was spiritually awakened with a serious question on my mind. In fact, it was in reference to an old gospel song I used to croon back in the day as a solo. Well, the Holy Spirit brought it back to remembrance; it was this question, in a song by my homeboys from St. Louis, Missouri, The O'Neal Twins, "World's Greatest Gospel Duo", and this scripture (Romans 12:1, KJV) which is My Personal Testimony!!! "All I Can Render"

> ♪♪What shall I Render - to God? What shall I give Him – in return?
> What shall I sacrifice - for an offering? Oh what shall I say...
> To express my thanks and gratitude to Thee,
> All I can render is my life...
>
> Lord, When I was lost –You found me.
> When I was sick–You healed my body.
> When I was hungry – Lord, You fed me.
> Lord, you've been mighty good..."♪

Family, He's (God) been so good; how can we express our thanks and gratitude to Thee; all we can Render (to God) is Our Life! As I was writing out this message; spiritually, my thoughts were just maybe, some, if not many of you are asking the same question too; and prayerfully, have the same answer. "What Shall I Render – to God?" All I Can Render is My Life! Hallelujah!

Somewhere along the lines, instead of serving divine love, peace and joy, the world's church is serving hate, grudges, faultfinding and human opinions. Is this false doctrine? Calvary have been wiped out of the way and instead become content with shaking the preacher's hand and being baptized in water. Some ministers will talk about anything but the story of the "Old Rugged Cross," and they will not recognize Calvary as the source of supply needed to pay all the debts to mankind that must be paid by those who claim they are going to Heaven anyhow... Some preach about the Gospel instead of preaching the Gospel. Even Paul Said: "And the ministry, which I have received of the Lord Jesus, to testify the gospel of the grace of God (Acts 20:24, KJV)." Yes, we are in the world, but not of the world. And yes, we are peculiar but we're not strange. Thank God I'm not in those numbers. Help us Lord?

Who defines you/us? Or should I ask, who or what do you allow to define you? Who defines who you are? In today's world there are countless forces and influences that try to define who we are. We all remember: "We've all been called everything but a Child of God." Also, "Sticks and stones can break your bones, but words can never hurt you...unless you believe them. Then, they destroy you." But because of who we are (Children of God) and whose we are (Christ's) in God's Kingdom, it's okay... In Mark 13 KJV, Jesus asked His Disciples, "Who do men say that I Am?" Claiming to be like Him, if someone would ask you the same, "Who do people say that you are?" What would your answer be? Would it possibly be anyone of the following or all of the following?

> *Kingdom Man or Woman
> *Soldier in the Army of God
> *Mighty Warrior
> *Prayer Warrior
> *Child of God
> *Encouraged Believer
> *Follower of Jesus
> *Disciple of Christ
> *Christ-Like (CHRISTian)
> *A King of the Lamb
> *Possessor of Life
> *Member of the Body
> *Branch of the True Vine
> *Redeemed Sinner

Yes, we've been called many things; we've allowed many names to be placed on us. But if the shoes (names) above fit, wear them proudly. If we're talking the talk, should we also walk the walk? So again, who defines you? 'JESUS!' Not man, Not the world... And because of who we really are and whose we truly are; what else would people call us or define us as? I may have forgotten a few names... Make your own list?

Jesus! Is it a necessity to know Him, and not know about Him? If we claim to personally, sincerely, and truly know Him, should we also know about Him? Because God loves us, He sent His Son Jesus to redeem man (us) back to Him. Because Jesus loved us, He gave His life on the cross at Calvary. If we love Him like He loves us, should we render (Serve God) our life to Him? Jesus didn't primarily serve the people within the four walls of the Synagogue; He ventured out to where the people were, (weddings, etc...). He engaged in itinerant ministry throughout Galilee, Judea, and many places between them. How is our ministry? Where are we serving? Who's leading us? As His Followers and Believers, we must go beyond the four walls of the visible local church just like Jesus did. (♪♫"To Be Like Jesus") God desires us to venture out by faith and see Him move. Let's be led by the Spirit and stop being afraid to follow. ♪♫"I Have Decided To Follow Jesus..."

Has anyone ever asked themselves or wondered what God is preparing them for? Or, have Prepared Me/You/Us for? (Prepared People) Are we being prepared to teach, preach, minister, pray...? We know that "The effectual fervent prayer of a righteous man availeth much" (James 5:16, KJV). Are we being prepared to just be an example of Him to others? To be "doers of the word, and not hearers only..." (James 1:22, KJV). In our preparation phase, we understand the importance of being prepared for life's storms. God is preparing each of us to know Him and to know Christ as our Savior; to treasure His word in our heart; to make prayer a vital part of our daily life; and to practice His presence daily in our life. He is also preparing us to receive His blessings and be in His favor. Again, understanding that God does the planning; we do the preparing. Realizing all life is a preparation to meet God - especially My Life. What about Yours? Ezekiel 38:7, KJV tells us to: "Be Prepared and Prepare Ourselves" Jesus said being prepared is very important for living the Christian life. In John 14:3 (KJV) Jesus also said: "If I go and Prepare a place for you, I will come again and receive you to myself, that where I am, there you may be also." Preparing involves calling upon the Lord, having a Godly relationship, praying, studying, and seeking the Lord with all our heart. Again, Jesus said, "I have gone to prepare a place for you." (Heaven) (John 14:2, KJV) He's preparing a "Prepared Place" for His "Prepared People." How Prepared are You/We?

I assume we all understand Physical and Spiritual Healthcare. There are two types of illness or hurts; some illness are not our fault, some we cause on our own... like eating too much or not eating a healthy diet, or being stressed out by strongholds. Yet, we want God to choose, shape, mold and use us. How can we be useful if were not fit physically not to mention, spiritually. Of course, God can use us either way because He is God. We should/must be healthy physically and spiritually; they both correlate. Most, if not all of us identify ourselves as Soldiers in the Army of the Lord. We know that a wounded soldier cannot do very much on the battlefield. Oh yes, we want to work in the vineyards but we cannot work if we are spiritually crippled (wounded).

We cannot work if we are impeded by anything that won't allow us to work, that won't allow us to March in the Army, that won't allow us to Run this Race, or simply Work in the Vineyards for the Lord. I don't know about you but I want to work and I am ready to work. I want my mind to be spiritually RIGHTeous and my body to be physically fit (healthy) to fight as a (Armored Up) soldier on the battlefield. I'm not afraid to fight as I've heard legendary gospel singers and pioneers; The Caravans tell me that ♪♫"God Don't' Want No Coward Soldiers." I'm not afraid to go out into the Vineyards. I'm not afraid to go down in the Valley; because I'd have Him (Jesus) with me. We (You/Me) are not afraid and we must also be fit to fight the strongholds of our lives. I want to be fit, not afraid, and available to go where God tells (He/Holy Spirit Leads) me to go. "Here I Am Lord, Send Me" Who's ready to be SENT – not went?

At times, as in Isaiah 6:1-8 (KJV), we need to be reminded that while visiting God's House (our local church), we "Enter to Worship and Depart to Serve." Every so often, we (some of us) make statements (opinions or complaints) that are saturated with self, as if WORSHIP is all about us. There are many times we, (some of us) have left a Worship Service only to complain or criticize: - "I didn't get anything out of the service today!"

"Why can't we sing less and pray more?"
"I don't think the preacher should've talked about this or that!"
"I can't believe he or she sat where I usually sit!"
"I can't believe the service was so long, I had somewhere else to be!"
"It's too many cell phones being used in the Church."

Here's the problem: Worship isn't about getting anything; it's about giving everything to God! The above attitudes or complaints make us idle judges of activity rather than active participants in adoration toward an Almighty Holy God. I hope we all know that Our Life's Purpose is to Reflect Christ and Our Life's Priority is to Resemble Christ. It's Not About You! It's Not About Me! It's Not About Us! It's All About Jesus!

Recently, I was looking at the man in the mirror - ME. As I gazed, I silently asked myself, "Am I really living for Christ?" Is He pleased with my service? I began to consciously question myself on whether or not I was content while living for Christ; while living a Godly, Favorable, Righteous and Spirit-led good life that's pleasing only to God. And was I satisfied with where I was in my Faith-Walk and in Christ? Hallelujah! I'm elated to respond, to testify, and to share with everyone that I am happy! Very! I'm happily living in the body, exhibiting fruitful labor. And that I am So Blessed and Highly Favored. If any of us were to sum up what our life is all about in one word, what would that word be? For me, (as it was also for Apostle

Paul in Philippians 1:21 KJV), that word would be CHRIST! Because for me, living is Christ and dying is gain. I am alive (in Christ) any I'm truly blessed. Yes, it's much easier for me to live, now that I'm in Christ and He's in me. Detroit, Michigan's own, The Clark Sisters - an American gospel vocal group along with the Holy Spirit reminds me that I'm livin' - I'm livin' it up!

♪♫"I like livin' this kinda life - I'm livin' a blessed life
I like livin' this kinda life - I'm livin' a blessed life
Ohhh I'm blessed... and highly favored. I'm livin'." How yawl livin'?

It's inevitable that we are constantly faced with the everyday trials and tribulations of life. There's a lot going on and it's nothing new. Family, please join me in Prayer? "Lord, I praise and thank you for your great love for me. Thank you for delivering me over and over again. Thank you for hearing my cry. Lord, thank you for the sufficiency of your grace (unmerited favor) (Ephesians 1:6, KJV), and your act of mercy (forgiveness). I thank you for Jesus and the "Helper" (John 14:16, KJV). Thank You Lord!" Amen.

Repeatedly, biblical writers have warned us against (Satan) the Devil. Peter calls him our "adversary" and "a roaring lion seeking whom he may devour" (1 Peter 5:8, KJV); 1 John 3:8, KJV says that Satan seeks to elicit sin in our lives to become like Him; and, In Matthew 13:39 (KJV), Jesus flat-out called the Devil "our enemy." Satan (the Devil), has declared war on us. He assaults our local churches, Our homes, Our families, Our marriages, Our youth, Our very minds; and, Our very being. So, isn't it time we declare war? War on the Devil! I believe all of us already know that we're in a War. We battle every day nonstop. It's a battle between the flesh and the Spirit. "For we wrestle (battle) not against flesh and blood, but against principalities, against powers, against the rulers of the darkness of this world, against spiritual wickedness in high places" (Ephesians 6:12, KJV). Yes, daily we have many battles in this war. The question is Who's Winning The Most (battles), Flesh vs. Holy Spirit? If we're not seriously preparing or is prepared for these battles, we will definitely lose most, if not all of them. Myself, I love to win. That's why I've read in Ephesians 6:10-13, KJV; and I've listened to Paul's battle cry: "Finally, be strong in the Lord and in the power of his might. Put on the whole armor of God that you may be able to stand against the schemes of the devil. For we do not wrestle against flesh and blood, but against the rulers, against the authorities, against the cosmic powers over this present darkness, against the spiritual forces of evil in the heavenly places. Therefore take up the whole armor of God that you may be able to withstand in the evil day, and having done all, to stand firm." We must stand and fight. It's a must if we are to survive and be victorious. We have great support (The Trinity) on our left and right flanks;

even at our rear because our Armor doesn't cover our backs - God got our backs. I don't know about you, but I am encouraged and I am brave; I know God don't want and He don't need, ♪♫"No Coward Soldiers" No, I'm not running away from these battles, but I am running for King Jesus.

I assume many of us speak daily to our spouses, children, co-workers, church members, etc.; how are we communicating with them, are we edifying? Ephesians 4:29 (KJV) tells us to: "Let no corrupt communication proceed out of your mouth, but that which is good to the use of edifying, that it may minister grace unto the hearers." Should we speak anytime in a corruptive manner? Are we gossiping (instead of Gospel)? We're supposed to be renewed in the spirit of our mind; remember it's no longer me/us but Him that is within me/us. We are now redeemed, born again... Ephesians 4:22–24 (ESV) tells us "to put off your old self, which belongs to your former manner of life and is corrupt through deceitful desires, and to be renewed in the spirit of your minds, and to put on the new self, created after the likeness of God in true righteousness and holiness." So, if we follow Jesus then we should believe Him when He said, "It is not what goes into the mouth that defiles a man, but what comes out of the mouth, this defiles a man" (Matthew 15:11 ESV). Corruption is confusing and God is not the author of confusion (1 Corinthians 14:33 KJV); and He is not corrupt, He's a Just God! A Righteous God!

"What's Love Got To Do With It?" American icon and musical Artist, Tina Turner's 1984 song is powerful. Hence, true love for God is not just going to a denominational church on a weekly basis, it's not just saying I love the Lord; I love Jesus; or, reading the scriptures every day. It's not just about being on the prayer line or attending bible study, Sunday school, etc... Those of us who truly and unconditionally loves God is going to have an affectionate reverence and an honoring attitude towards Him; with a passionate love for His Son and an unwavering obedience to the Holy Spirit. I don't know about you but I am so elated, I'm overwhelmed; and rightly so, because of Who I am in HIM and Whose I am - HIS! I am so grateful for what He's done for me, to me, and through me. Are you? I am also thankful to be blessed with His (God's) Favor. Are you? I can honestly say that I Love Him and I'm justly showing Him - and I will continue to show Him every day of my life. What about you? God says, "If you love me, you will keep my commandments" (John 14:15, NRSV). We know that the greatest commandment which is, "Love the Lord your God with all your heart, mind and soul" (Matthew 22:38, KJV). We also know talk is cheap; so, let us began showing it moreover than say it. Action does speak louder than words. Besides, the Love of God will speak for itself. God has showed that He loves us. What are we showing Him? God does Love us; now, do we love God? Have a Loving day!

Family, the Lord has declared war on carnality, sin, addiction, depression, and fear. He has declared war against the powers of Satan that destroy our lives. And He's calling each of us to join in the battle and willingly offer ourselves to the fight. I'm in. And, I'm with Him. Are you on the Lord's side? If we've just been sitting back watching, it's time to stop being a spectator and start being a warrior, a soldier and join in the fight. We're now realizing that we are fighting for our Salvation. It's unfortunate that some of us may not think we're in a war zone, but we are. We are on the front lines of a spiritual war that started back with Adam and Eve. We're facing an enemy whose goal is to kill, steal, and destroy. He is a crafty opponent, not one to be underestimated. Yes, even though we're not of this world; this world we're in is a war zone; and we as Soldiers in the Army of the Lord are to get ready, watch and pray, be alert, and stay ready for war. Are You Ready? We are definitely at war; and surely, we're in a spiritual battle. We're in a battle for our mind, because our greatest asset is our mind; and that battle is vicious, it's intense, it is unrelenting, and it is unfair because Satan never plays fair. This violent battle is raging around us twenty-four hours per day, nonstop. It's good to know that Jesus is presently accepting new brave recruits to fight in this battle. I've accepted Christ and in the process, I've accepted to be a soldier! ♪♪"I'm a Soldier in the Army of the Lord" Are You? There is a War Against the People of God! The good news is Jesus wins this war in the end; and, We Have The Victory! ♪♪"Victory Is Mine!" Hallelujah!

One summer morning in June, I was abruptly awakened by an inspiring strong gospel song. I wouldn't be surprised if this possibly have happened to anyone of you. Anyway, I couldn't get this (encouraging) song out of my mind. It had quickly become deeply embedded in my spirit. Why, I didn't know at the time until the Holy Spirit enlightened me. Because of all I had been going through, and even as I was struggling through issues at that very moment; this Gospel song by William Becton and Friends was telling me to, ♪♪"Be Encouraged, No matter what's going on; He'll (Jesus) make it alright, but I got to stay strong. And for me to Hold on, and that trouble don't last always; and that these trials are just a test of my faith." Realizing that in our faith walk with God, He will test us every now and then. Sounds encouraging to you? The parts (lyrics) of the song that spiritually uplifted and inspired me the most was, for me to "Be Encouraged" and to "Be Strong and Stay Strong" (Ephesians 6:10, KJV). Yes, scriptures tells us we'll have storms, we'll have trials and tribulations, we'll have lots of stress and drama; yet, still, we must ♪♪"Be Encouraged!" We have to be! God will work it out, if we just believe. And also, let's remember Psalm 30:5, KJV: "Weeping may endure for a night, but joy cometh in the morning!" Family, ♪♪"Be Encouraged" God's Got You!

In times of illness, cordially, we've all been told to rest and heal. We are grateful. When Peter wrote about Jesus' bearing our sins on the cross, he referred to Isaiah 53:5, KJV which says, "With His wounds we are healed," but was it only in the context of spiritual healing? Yes, someone somewhere is resting and slowly recovering from their personal physical illness; and, has grown stronger in Him spiritually. Myself, I'm not one who believes every time we get sick it's God's way of saying slow down, it's time to quit or it's a punishment. But being sick and pressing through it is a great time to remember God's grace; and, I have. I pray you have too! Yes, I am weak but thou art strong! As God spoke to Paul in 2 Corinthians 12:9-10 RSV; and it seems now God is speaking to us saying: "My grace is sufficient for you, for my power is made perfect in weakness. Therefore I will boast all the more gladly in my weakness, so that the power of Christ may rest upon me. For the sake of Christ, then, I am content with weakness... For when I am weak, then I am strong." So, through it all, I've learned to ask the Lord to work and move in me - in spite of my physical condition and to constantly endow me with His Spirit. He hasn't disappointed me yet! If you ask, neither will He you. I suggest the next time you're sick - rest up, drink plenty fluids, follow doctor's orders, take your meds, pray, read the word and expect big things... it worked for me! Besides, John 9:4 KJV tells me: "I must work the works of Him that sent me, while it is day: the night cometh, when no man can work." Hallelujah!

Some of us truly believe that Salvation, Eternal Life, The Lamb's Book of Life, The Lake of Fire (Revelation 20:15, KJV) and Judgement Day is a very serious matter. Do we really know how serious? We say and proclaim that we are born again; that we are saved; that we've changed, that we are Believers and we Follow Christ. We're not just talking, are we? We're not just a show to the world. Hypocritically speaking, are we talking the talk and not walking the walk. The Godfather of Soul (James Brown) says, "We're Talking Loud and Saying Nothing" And R&B Group Cameo says we're "Talking Out The Side of Our Necks." Someone said, "Once Saved, Always Saved." Well, who saved you? If God saved you, you can't lose it because it depends on God. If you saved yourself, you can lose it because it depends on you. Your salvation is eternally secure if God did the saving. It's all about FAITH! Faith involves an act of commitment and trust, in which we commit our life to Jesus Christ and trust Him alone as our Savior and Lord. Faith is essential for salvation. It's believing, hearing and living the word. It's that commitment to Jesus as Savior and Lord. It is a personal and individual decision and our faith walk. It is faith in the promises of God that all who trust in Christ will not perish but have eternal life (John 10:28-30, KJV). So; Salvation, The Book of Life, The Lake of Fire, Being Born Again, Being Saved, Atonement, Repentance, Redemption, and Eternal Life... ARE YOU SERIOUS?

Early one morning I was awakened by the Holy Spirit with this particular song/message; "He that hath an ear, let him hear what the Spirit saith unto the Churches." "We're Crossing Over" Yes, this song ♪♪"We're crossing over one by one; (We're moving on...) We're fast approaching life's setting sun; (Don't let Him catch you...) Don't let Him catch you with your work undone... We're crossing over; (We're crossing over one by one). (Isaiah 55:6-7, KJV) tells us to: "Seek ye the Lord while He may be found" so we shouldn't let anybody turn us around.

No, we should let Satan block our path; and, we shouldn't let the sun go down on our wrath. We're crossing over one by one; (We're moving on...) We're fast approaching life's setting sun. Don't let Him catch you...Don't let Him catch you with your work undone. We're crossing over one by one. John 9:4 KJV tells me: "I must work the works of Him who sent me while it is day; the night is coming when no one can work" The Kingdom of God is moving. As the Church we must transition. Like the Disciples, let us prepare ourselves to follow Christ and cross over, (Matthew 8:18-22 NIV). Remember, we're just pilgrims traveling through.

Is it just me? Sometimes in meditation and in humbleness I say Lord, You Know. Lord, You Know all about me, You Know what I'm going through; with my health, my finances, my family, my overall trials and circumstances, even my faith-walk, (Psalm 139:1-5, KJV). Yes, I pray leaving it all at the Altar for you Lord. Daily, I'm learning more each day to Trust you Lord and not lean to my own or anyone else's understanding. Spiritually, in thought and meditation, I'm elated because it's comforting to know that God Knows; He knows me, and, He got me! Lord, You Know.

It's Religious vs. Righteous! Based on the King James Version of the Bible, the word "**religion**" I believe is mentioned only 5 times: (Acts 26:5 Galatians 1:13 Galatians 1:14 James 1:26 James 1:27, KJVs). And in the King James version of the Bible the word "**righteous**" is mentioned/appears 238 times, "**righteousness**" is mentioned/appears 302 times, and "**righteously**" is mentioned/appears 8 times. Religious vs. Righteous! Which are we? Did someone say that they were a very religious person? What do religious people do? They find out where religious things are happening in the religious world. They hang around and do those notable religious things so they can add them to their religious resumes. They are devout, traditional religious believers that oftentimes quench the Holy Spirit. Question, should religious leaders and believers stop hiding behind their religion? Umm! So, what do RIGHTEOUS people do? They live to glorify God and God alone. They are filled with the Holy Spirit and they sing only one song: ♪♪"Make me an instrument; an instrument of blessing, all for the glory of your name."♪ You know they live prayerful lives; they study and grow in the Word, they wait on the Lord to direct them to souls perishing so they can share their faith or be used to heal the sick and dying. They are led and they live life obedience to God's Will.

The sacrifices of a Righteous life is a life set apart, a peculiar life, cleansed, purged, and sanctified to produce fruit and good works of faith. Let us not miscalculate the difference between being religious and righteous. Are we religious-minded or Spiritual-minded? God's word says that to be religious-minded is death (Romans 8: 6, KJV) and to be spiritually minded is life and peace. Religious-minded people want miracles and power. Spiritual-minded people want wisdom and truth. For the Bible reveals "He Himself bore our sins in His body on the cross, that we might die to sin and live to RIGHTEOUSNESS; for by His wounds you were healed" (1 Peter 2:24, KJV). Note, it didn't say Religiousness. Matthew 5:8, KJV tells us "None but the righteous (pure in heart) shall see god" also, Psalm 11:7 KJV says, "For the righteous Lord loveth righteousness; His countenance doth behold the upright." Yes! ♪♫"None But The Righteous" - So, we have a choice; what will we be, Religious or Righteous? Please, allow God to cover you with the robe of Righteousness, (Isaiah 61:10, KJV) and be blessed. Family, choose Righteousness and be Righteous!

What if our hearing and reading the word is not enough? What if hearing the preacher preach or the teacher teach isn't enough? What if Bible Study, Sunday school or Prayer Meetings isn't enough? Then what is??? Seriously, take a look around you; c'mon, open your eyes and observe your surroundings, just observe? We are living in an ungodly world. This sinful world is vividly displaying lies, hatred, injustice, deceitfulness, lust and so on... Sadly, it's appalling. Do we, or should we accept these things that are going on in the world? 1 John 2:15-16, KJV tells us to "Love not the world, neither the things that are in the world..." So, what is there left to do??? Assemble, attend to grow! Where are we now? Where do we go from here? I know I'm preaching to the choir. My Lord! Can someone please enlighten me/us? (Matthew 22:37-39, KJV). Thank you Jesus!

Are we all created in the image and likeness of God? Yes we are! 2 Corinthians 3:18 (ISV) says, "As all of us reflect the glory of the Lord with unveiled faces, we are becoming more like Him with ever-increasing glory by the Lord's Spirit." I would hope so. ♪♫"He is Lord!" So, if Moses can reflect the glory of God after meeting with Him, we, (you and I) can also reflect His glory by meeting with Him in worship. Moses experienced outward transformation when he saw the glory of God. As Christians, we (you and I) can enjoy inward transformation when we see the same glory. By working through His Holy Spirit, God will complete the work of salvation in our hearts and lives. I sincerely believe that Spiritual Transformation is the very purpose of our life on Earth. What else is life but a series of lessons to learn, teachable moments, and an ongoing opportunity to evolve and fulfill our Godly potential as spiritual beings? Spiritually, we're not of this world; and, we are not to be conformed to this world, but be transformed by the renewing of our mind. So Family, ♪♫"Be Transformed!"

Anyone feel like running for Jesus? ♪♫"I'm pressing on the upward way, New heights I'm gaining every day; Still PRAYING as I onward bound," Philippians 3:14, KJV tells us to "PRESS toward the mark for the prize of the high calling of God in Christ Jesus." When we Pray we should also continue Pressing. P.R.E.S.S. - **P**ray, **R**ely on God, **E**xalt yourself (to a higher rank or power), **S**anctify yourself, and **S**alvation is yours. (P.R.E.S.S.) In Christ, we must faithfully proceed or move forward with a since of urgency. Time is running out! You know we got to stand on His Word and we got to Pray! Some, if not all of us are living witnesses that

Prayer works. It changes people, things and circumstances. Yes it does! Prayer is essential to our Salvation. Jesus knew the importance of teaching the Disciples how to pray "The Lord's Prayer." In 1 Thessalonians 5:17, KJV Paul tells us to "Pray without ceasing." It should be a big part of our lifestyle. We should never stop praying. Keep praying through smooth or tough situations. Good or bad times. God will answer. God is able. We trust, we believe, now we know what we must do: P.U.S.H. **P**ray **U**ntil **S**omething **H**appens. I'm reminded of a 1964 single by The Impressions ♪♪"Keep On Pushing" Keep on pushin' - Keep on pushin' - I've got to keep on pushin' Hallelu-jah, Hallelu-jah, Keep on pushin'♪Yes, we must "Keep on Pushin'" until something happens. And we must also P.R.E.S.S. and keep on "Pressing Towards The Mark" as we P.U.S.H. and "Keep on Pushin'" Pray Until Something Happens; and it will! Are there any witnesses?

Metaphorically, our life is a Book. In the Chapters of our Book, it'll show we're all living either an acceptable or unacceptable life, according to God. It may also show our lives as being religious or righteous; and, the contents will either be the Gospel or full of gossip. We all have sinned and fallen short; therefore, we all have a Story to share or not to share. Our Story has a beginning and an ending. We are the writers and that means we are the personal Authors of our book. Looking at the cover (me) of My Book, you may or may not form an opinion. The (my) outward appearance of My Book is not an indicator of the real me; or, does it justify who I am. No! "You can't judge My Book by its cover."

Each of us know our Book's personal contents and no one knows it better than we do; each page listing the trials, tribulations, hardships, storms, valleys, mountains, transgressions and backsliding, etc. The Story content of our book should not be considered a Novel or Textbook; it should define itself according to our Spiritual and intellectual relationship with God the Father, Jesus the Son and The Holy Spirit. I don't know Your Story or about Your Book; but F.Y.I., the design content of My Book includes a sequence of various actions and elements such as Sin, Redemption, Forgiveness, Growth, Grace, Worship, Praise, Prayer, Faith and The Trinity. I thank God My Book is readable because of what it illustrates when read; thanks to the illustrator, (the Holy Spirit). I am proud and not ashamed of My Book. Each Chapter is a testament to who I am and whose I am, (My Testimony).

I'm blessed to have My Book marketed by the Publisher, Jesus Christ. No, you don't know My Story but if you're really interested in finding out and you'd like to read a good Book, Great! No, it's not 'The Good Book,' it is an open book. I believe the Chapters are very uplifting! While reading, you'll find out that I am not the star of My Book, although for a long time I thought I was. Yes, I thought I had it going on. Not! Also while reading, you will find out that I was quite a character, but I wasn't the Main Character. "Not I, but He that was within me," and I didn't know it... No, I didn't have a clue. Who knows, Your Book may be somewhat similar to mine, especially some Chapters! Prayerfully, you have the same Illustrator and Publisher! It's inevitable, that someday My Book will be closed permanently; it will conclude. Presently, it's being summarized… But for now, it's an opened Book for however long God wants and allows it to be publicly opened for reading. With life's blessings, redemption, atonement and forgiveness through HIM, I'd say it could possibly be a #1 Seller. Nevertheless, it is a good read. I'd recommend it to anyone. Now, what's yawl's story? Yes, your life is a Book too. So, who's the Publisher of Your Life's Book?

All who proclaim/profess to be of Christ, ask your selves, is this message for me? **Pastors/ Preachers**; preach the word, live the word. **Teachers** (including me); teach the word, live the word. **Ministers**; minister the Gospel, live the Gospel. **Evangelists;** evangelize God's word, live God's word. **Prayer Warriors**; pray God's Promises (His word) back to Him, live His Promises. **Choirs/Everyone**; Sing God's Praises, live God's Praises. **Christ-like Believers**; believe God's word, live and act on His word. Any and all readers and hearers as of God's word, live it. It's your choice. "All who has an ear let them hear what the Spirit saith unto the Church." Can you hear Him now?

True love for God is not just going to church on a weekly basis; it's not just saying I love God; or, reading the scriptures every day. It's not just about being on the prayer line or attending bible study or prayer meetings… Those of us who truly love God are going to do just about all of what's been mentioned. Yes, all of that and then some… And, they're also going to have an affectionate reverence and an honoring attitude towards Him (God); with a passionate love for His Son and an unwavering obedience to the Holy Spirit. Well Lord, I'm runnin', tryin' to make a hundred because I know that (99½) ninety-nine and a half won't do. That's why I am so elated and overwhelmed because of Who I am in HIM and Whose I am - HIS! I am also grateful for what He's done for me, to me, and through me. Yes, I am thankful to be blessed with (God's) Favor. Are you? As I've grown in Grace, I can honestly say that I Love Him and I am attempting towards showing Him daily. What about you? Yawl be blessed, and while you're at it, be a blessing - to someone. Now excuse me while I get My Praise on? You're on your own…

Question, is it just me or is it everyone who love to talk? Most of us do love to talk. We talk to our best friends, significant other, Facebook, FaceTime, Psychologists, Psychiatrists, Family and/or Marriage Counselors, and even to ourselves. Yes, we talk a lot. We talk to everyone under the sun. Is there someone who any of us can call upon at any hour, day or night? And will they answer and talk with us - about anything and everything, in confidence? No!? So, when was the last time any of Us ♪♪"Had a little talk with Jesus"? God is concerned about each and every detail of our lives. He wants us to talk to Him and He wants to talk to each of us about the everyday things of life. Let's indulge in a conversation with God, even if to just Listen. God is right now saying to someone, somewhere ♪♪"I Miss My Time With You" (Our one-on-one time)... Is it you? Yawl please excuse me, I've 3 visitors waiting to talk and fellowship with me. You may just know them as well.

Sin is no joke to God. God takes sin very seriously. Sin is so serious that it cost God's begotten Son, Jesus Christ, His very life. If God takes sin that seriously, shouldn't we as well? Romans 3:24 (KJV) tells us "For all have sinned, and come short of the glory of God;" Yes, we've all fallen short, and yes, while we were still sinners God saved us, but that does not mean the realm of sin is where we stay. Am I a sinner? "We're all sinners saved by grace." So, how shall we who died to sin still live in it (Romans 6:2, KJV)...? Romans 6:7, KJV also says: "for he who has died is freed from sin." and 1 Peter 4:1,(KJV) tells us that Christ died so that we may be dead to sin. So, let us consider ourselves to be dead to sin, but alive to God in Christ Jesus, (Romans 6:11, KJV). "In whom we have redemption through His blood, the forgiveness of sins, according to the riches of His grace;" ♪♪"What can wash away my sin? Nothing but the blood of Jesus!" Now, ♪♪"I Am Redeemed!" To God Be The Glory!

Pastors, Teachers, Evangelists, Apostles, Preachers who plant and water; we're all described as ministers, servants or attendants of the Word of God. Never forgetting "Whose we are, and whom we serve". That we have faith and we have work to do. And because of our faith in God, our work has been appointed by God. Our work precedes the increase by God. Apostle Paul reminds us when he says, "I have planted, Apollos watered; but God gave the increase." Yes, we are laborers! (1 Thessalonians 2:9, KJV) No, we cannot change or save anyone or anybody. Upon giving the Word (preaching or teaching), we're to be steadfast (1 Corinthians 15:58, KJV). Yes, we are filled and led by the Holy Spirit; He puts it on us and we put it to the people. Acknowledging that as minister's our abilities and gifts, no matter the differences have been given and ordained by God - as we all are engaged in one great work. Also, as Ministers of the Gospel, (Pastors, Preachers, Teachers, Apostles, Evangelists) not only should we be "one in Christ Jesus", but we should also be one in having the same work, the same relationship to God, and the same relationship to the Church. Also, we should be of one mind with regard to the great objectives we must always have before us – that God will be glorified, and Christ have the preeminence in all things; that sinners will be saved, believers sanctified, and the cause of Christ advanced. So, as Ministers what do we do? We go on in the work of planting and watering the seed. Can we hope for fruit? Will there be an increase? It is only by the power of God that there will be an increase. Except the Lord will give the increase, their labour will be in vain (1 Corinthians 3:6-8, KJV). So, Who's giving the increase? (Holy Ghost) Yes, God is calling each of us as Ministers to continue diligently in the great work He lays upon us, planting and watering while we have the opportunity, and waiting on the Lord for the increase; especially that of preaching the gospel and teaching the truth. We understand that

God alone is to be glorified in the resulting increase. Let's be real, let's be obedient, let's go to work planting and watering the Word of God, the good seed of the Kingdom. "Preach the Word!" (2 Timothy 4:2, KJV) "Preach the Gospel!" (Mark 16:15, KJV) and (1 Corinthians 1:17, KJV) Thank God, I'm His Servant, His Teacher planting and watering through these written messages. The increase, God's got it. Hallelujah!

Thankfulness is an expression of gratitude. It is the sincere exaltation of God through praise, worship and witness. "Oh give thanks to the Lord, for He is good; for His steadfast love endures forever!" (1 Chronicles 16:34, KJV). Some, if not many of us, often pray asking God for something. Without hesitation, we ask Him for self or someone else. Family, can you please pause and join me in just thanking God for being God?

> Lord, I Thank You for your blessings, so that I may bless others...
> Lord, I Thank You for forgiving me, now I must forgive others...
> Lord, I Thank You for loving me, now I can in spite of - love others...
> Lord, I Thank You for your majesty; how majestic is your name. Now I can also look forward to hearing your voice from your Majestic Glory on high as Jesus did; you saying, "This is my Son, whom I love; with Him, I am well pleased."
> "Lord, I Thank You. Amen."

Unfortunately, there's been no other time whereas our country is in a constitutional crisis. Presently, our democracy is being tested; challenged by the 45th President of the United States. Because of him, are your morals and values via the Fruits of the Spirit in jeopardy? Is your faith also being tested? Because of the corruption, conspiracies, dishonesty, injustice, aggressive family separation policies, racism, unethical righteousness and treason of any politician (to name a few); so has hatred and sin corrupted your mind. Is your transformed and renewed mind under siege? Or, have you lost your joy? Jesus is love and because of Him being within me, "hate has no place in my (life/heart) faith-walk."

We should not allow hate or sinful behavior of anyone dictate our faith in God or steer us off the path of righteousness. That type of behavior is not pleasing to God; it's a "sin against the Gospel," besides we're to proclaim "The Gospel." Don't let any political rhetoric or gossip replace "The Gospel!" Each of us (everyone) will give an account of ourselves to God; yes, God will hold us all accountable. All of us will have to stand before God. 2 Corinthians 5:10, KJV say: "For we must all appear before the judgment seat of Christ, so that each of us may receive what is due us for the things done while in the body, whether good or bad." Please Family, don't allow the Devil or anyone else steal your Joy! In John 15:11 KJV, Jesus says: "These things have I spoken unto you, that my joy might remain in you, and that your joy might be full." The joy you and I have as a Believer/Christian is the joy of Jesus. It (True Joy) can only be found in Jesus, not unbelief, not fame, not success, not pleasure, and certainly not a politician! Besides, it's the opposite of everything that Jesus stands for! Love is the answer… So focus (stay focused) on Jesus and not on anyone else. Hallelujah! ♪♪♪"This Joy…." ♪

As we daily go about living in our comings and goings, take a moment (now) to personally ask yourselves with sincerity, "Am I truly pleasing God?" Or; ask this, "Am I in God's Will?" Maybe ask this one, "Is God pleased with my Servanthood?" And lastly, "Am I personally satisfied with where I am spiritually in Christ Jesus?" Some of you may know or may not know the answer to any one of these, if not all of these, but God does. I'm praying you honestly know. Lord knows I'm also praying you find out! Please, don't fool yourselves? There is always an easy path and a RIGHT PATH in everyone's life; especially in our life's Faith-Walk. It's our choice. Again, just ask yourselves one or all of these questions? Now, what's next? Read the King James Translations of: (Romans 12:1-2) * (Proverbs 16:9) and (Proverbs 20:24).

If we Fellowship with Christ, we have a Relationship with Him. Because of my personal relationship, I know "I Can Do All Things Through Christ Who Strengthens Me" (Philippians 4:13, KJV). Other than my own life in Christ, I know that there are not many things in life that I can honestly guarantee; for instance, I do not know what will happen tomorrow. I do not know what will happen with the economy. I do not know what will happen with "wars and rumors of wars," I do not know what will happen with the new restrictive abortions laws passed in several states. I don't know what will happen with climate change. And no, I do not know what will happen with many things that aren't pleasing to me as a Believer and especially to God. But, I do know that every sinner who comes to Jesus by faith, repenting of his or her sins and accepting Him as Savior, will be saved by the grace of God. I do know "that at the name of Jesus every knee should bow, of things in heaven, and things in earth, and things under the earth; and that every tongue should confess that Jesus Christ is Lord, to the glory of God the Father" (Philippians 2:10-11, KJV). I truly know this because I have God's Word; because, His word shall not return void. Hallelujah!!!

Can we talk? I have an overwhelming sense of despair, and lack thereof over my struggle (problem) with sin, am I alone? Romans 7:14 (KJV) says, "For we know that the law is spiritual: but I am carnal, sold under sin." Okay, sin is complicated; but we can still forsake all efforts to serve God in the strength of our flesh, regardless. As "The Church," no one is exempt from sin; we all experience it but rarely talk about it abroad. Yes, we struggle. We know what's right and yet we still do what's wrong. We pray to God and ask forgiveness, yet we repeatedly transgress… As each one of us attempt/try to live righteously, we are confronted religiously with this dilemma. I thoroughly share Apostle Paul's confession; "I do not do the good I want, but the evil I do not want is what I keep on doing. … Wretched man that I am!" (Romans 7:19-24,

KJV)... After reading this scripture in it's entirely, I truly understand exactly what Paul is saying. I can see myself in it. Can you? I believe that in its present tense, it's mirroring the daily day after day personal experiences of my life. Speaking of the 'spirit vs. flesh' (inner warfare), it is unfortunate that there's no getting away (no escape) from it. The battles are definitely on. This war within causes us to struggle/wrestle (with sin) on the inside of us non-stop every single day. Did someone say that "I'm only human?" Yes, I am of flesh; yes, my flesh is weak; yes, my flesh is in "bondage to and overpowered by sin, but God! God is holy and He hates sin! And as long as we are human; in our mortal bodies, we will wrestle and struggle with sin. It's inevitable. Evangelist, Joyce Meyer said, "I may not be where I want to be, but thank God I am not where I used to be." And Former Slaver & Preacher, John Newton said, "I am not what I ought to be, I am not what I want to be, I am not what I hope to be in another world; but still I am not what I once used to be, and by the grace of God I am what I am." Sin is constantly knocking on our doors; our walk with Jesus is not easy; yet, it is a blessing, ♪♪"Cause Jesus paid it all, all to Him I owe, Sin had left a crimson stain..." ♪

Who believe Happiness depends on wealth, power, or status? What makes one Happiest in life may or may not be viewed by all the same way. Most, if not all have experienced Happiness through some form of service or generosity. Generously, if you didn't know, it's giving your life away for the sake of the Gospel. Our Obedient Faith makes each of us offer our lives as a living sacrifice and serve God by serving others. With this said, in Christ, our heart is happy! The Heart is the Happiest when we are serving God; when Love (Agape Love) is being shared or expressed; and, when someone is being blessed by God's tangible or non-tangible Love. The Heart is the Happiest when you're forgiven and, when you forgive. The Heart is the Happiest when you are Fruitful; and, when you show and exhibit the Fruits of the Spirit. The Heart is the Happiest when your Spirituality is made out of happiness, joy, peace and love (Romans 15:13, ASV). Happiness is a choice rather than a result of circumstances and surroundings. Being happy doesn't mean you are content. Seeking and having God in our decision-making and all of our life activities leads to Happiness of the Heart because this puts us in line with His (God's) Will for our lives. ♪♪"Because I'm Happy!" (Pharrell Williams). How's Your Heart?

In an earlier message, I shared with you about unimportant nonessential things I don't know. In fact, none of us should dwell on them. I also mentioned those essential things I do know and are crucial to my Soul Salvation, depicting who I am in Christ. We know that God is all knowing; and that we should get to Know Him. By nature, we assume to know things of this world, but we're not of the world. We're Pilgrims! Those things we assume to know and are somewhat proud of are not important to God and shouldn't be important to us. A wise man knows God and His Word, everything else is worldly debatable (nonessential). Here's A News Flash! There's no debating God's Word, "it shall not return unto Him void." Besides, this is what God commanded for us to Know. "The Gospel" (His Word), and spread it throughout the world (Great Commission). Yes, God's Word and His Promises is what I do know! God's Love is what I do know! Living the Fruits of the Spirit and being fruitful is what I do know. The Trinity is what I do know! My Soul and Eternal Life is seriously based on them; not things of this world. (2 Peter 3:18, KJV) * (1 Peter 1:25, KJV) Furthermore, it's good to "Know The Lord!" So, what essentially do you know?

Scripturally, Romans 3:24, KJV tells us "For all have sinned, and come short of the glory of God;" Yes, we've all fallen short; and yes, while we were still sinners God saved us, but that does not mean the realm of sin is where we stay. Am I a sinner. "We're all sinners saved by grace." So, how shall we who died to sin still live in it (Romans 6:2, KJV)...? Now Romans 6:7, KJV says: "for he who has died is freed from sin." 1 Peter 4:1, NIV reminds us that: "Christ Died to Make Us Dead to Sin." So let us consider ourselves to be dead to sin, but alive to God in Christ Jesus (Romans 6:11, KJV) * (1 Peter 4:1, KJV). "In whom we have redemption through his blood, the forgiveness of sins..." ♪♫"I Am Redeemed" To God be the Glory!

Does anyone believe as I? Through the years, I've grown in grace and in the knowledge of our Lord and Savior Jesus; in my ministry, I've learned through the guidance of the Holy Spirit, that I cannot Teach, if I haven't been Taught; I cannot Preach, if I haven't been Preached to; I cannot be a Testimony, if I don't have a Testimony; and, I cannot Speak or Live the Word, if I haven't Heard, Read or Grown in the Word. "He that has an ear let him hear." I've come to believe the Lord cannot and will not send one to preach healing while they themselves have not received the healing – thus, how can you tell people 'be healed in the Name of Jesus', and testify 'that Jesus is the healer' when He has not healed you? One cannot preach holiness yet they themselves look unholy and their deeds and what comes out of them is unholy. A Temple (person) whom Jesus Christ is dwelling in is holy inside and outside, otherwise a hypocrite. I also believe one cannot preach the gospel of Jesus Christ without knowing the Gospel (Good News). ♪♫"Get Right With God!" Be available, be shaped, be molded and be used. Personally, as a Servant and Living Sanctuary, I want to be in God's Favor; as I grow, know and be used.

At some point in time, we've all had health issues (sickness). As we continue health-wise on a path to fully recovering, we're beginning to regain our appetite. It's safe to say that many of us love to eat and we love tasting good, delicious food. We want just a taste to intrigue our appetite; and when it's so good, we want to share it with others. "C'mon, you gotta taste this!" Has anyone tried Jesus? "Taste and See how Good and Sweet God is?" "Try It, You Will Like It." Try Him? To taste means to eat, discern, perceive, or to evaluate. To Taste in its verb form refers to the testing of goods by means of the sense of taste. The Lord is available to us to try (taste) Him. So let us not hesitate any longer; come and enjoy, and magnify and exalt the Divine Name and Goodness of the Lord. He has challenged us to "**Taste**" and "**See**" that the

Lord is "**Good**" (Psalm 34:88, KJV). King David wanted the people to Taste the Goodness of God, because he wanted them to experience God first hand; I, as King David want the same. Yes, I've chosen Jesus to be the Lord of my life. I have tasted His goodness and it's (He's) better than Campbell Soup which is: "Mm! Mm! Good!" Now, is anyone hungry? I'm starving!

Family, I firmly believe we are never beyond God's grace, but if we truly want to experience it; that is, the full benefits of His grace, then we have to grow in it. God wants each of us to grow in the grace and knowledge of our Lord and Savior. For us to grow in grace means for us to increase in the likeness of Christ through the unmerited power of God's Spirit (Holy Spirit). I Peter 5:12 KJV, tells us that: "This is the true grace of God in which you stand." So we are *saved by grace* (Ephesians 2:8, KJV) and we *stand by grace* (Romans 5:2, KJV), and we *grow by grace*, (2 Peter 3:18, KJV). Grace is favour. In the Bible the word grace often implies a free gift. The grace of God is thus the favour of God, His free gift to us. Lastly, we must be cognizant that the command to "Grow in Grace" does not mean we will totally give up sin. That's where God's Grace comes in.

Our human nature lures us into carelessly taking things for granted, (God, His purpose for us, etc.). Every now and then we need to validate our relationship with the Triune. We should/ need to examine our faith-walk, our Servanthood; and revisit our New Covenant relationship between us and God mediated by Jesus. We shouldn't gamble with our Salvation. We should never assume we've arrived; or, become complacent or comfortable whereas we become remiss (negligent) in pleasing and serving God. We slack, become lazy and take shortcuts in doing what "thus saith the Lord" and at times quenching the Holy Spirit. We can overcome this. With a contrite heart, we need to love God zealously (Deuteronomy 6:5, RSV), remain steadfastly focused, never forgetting the great purpose He has for us. Never taking our eyes off the Prize (Philippians 3:14 RSV). We can/must do this!

C'mon Family, join me; let's take a moment to meditate and review our spiritual standing with the Lord? Let's take a personal look at our mindset, our attitude, our lifestyle, our fruits, our beliefs, and our covenant? Are we satisfied with most, if not all? Do we believe God is satisfied/pleased? Is there more - or, much work we have to do? No, I haven't arrived, have you? In an earlier message, I dialogued about HELP. Needing His Help (John 14:26, NKJV) to stay on the path of righteousness, to remain transformed by the renewing of the mind; and, to confirm my New Testament Covenant (Jesus). Now, I've only this to share... ♪♫"Lord, lead me, guide me along the way, for if you lead me I cannot stray. Lord let me walk each day with Thee. Lead me, oh Lord lead me?" Hallelujah! Now please excuse me while I meditate with My Help, the HELPER?

Other than attending weekly church services on Sunday, why do we have Bible Studies? Why do we have Revivals? Why do we have Sunday/Church Schools and Vacation Bible

Schools? Why do we have Prayer Meetings and Telephoned Prayer Lines? All of these are opportunities. Church attendance only on Sundays isn't enough. **Group Bible Study** is invaluable (Luke 6:12–16; Mark 4:34, KJVs). We must assemble, and we must have an understanding of God through His Word. It's crucial to know God, to become closer to Him. **Prayer** is more than edification; it's encouraging one another to endure - leading to change, and thus, our burdens aren't carried alone, (Galatians 6:2, KJV); (John 17:23, KJV). Prayer is also powerful and effective, whether Intercessory, Supplication or Thanksgiving! (1 Thessalonians 5:17, KJV); (Matthew 26:41, KJV); (1Timothy 2:1-4, KJV); (Philippians 4:6, KJV)... and the King James Versions of: (Acts 2:42); (Hebrews 10:25); (Galatians 5:13); (Luke 22:14-20); (Matthew 18:19-20; James 5:14-15); (Romans 10:17); and, (Romans 12:1). All of these scriptures validate WHY. I've no other explanation to share. It's your choice, your salvation. Now, who want to grow closer to Christ? (Stepping on any toes?)

When I look into the mirror, what do we see? Do I see a "Fake Christian?" Some of us might've heard the song: ♪♫"99½ Won't Do" No, it will not. I want to be all I can be in the Lord and totally all-in for the Lord - 100%! No half steppin' or short-stoppin'. Christ is real and He went all the way for us; can we go all the way for Him? Scriptures warn us about false prophets and false doctrines (Matthew 7:15 & Ephesians 4:14, KJVs). We should want nothing false or fake. Scriptures also says Jesus is the way, the truth, and the life (John 14:6, KJV); I want the Truth (3 John 1:4, KJV). I want to be pure (Holy), to walk in purity before the Lord. I don't want to live a lie, or my living to be in vain; I only want to live a Testimony. And, I don't want to be Fake in my faith-walk with Christ. No, I'm not perfect; no one is. I just don't want to hear a Sermon, I want to live it. So, what do people see when they look at you?

"Lord, when we gave our lives to you, we received your grace and we are expected to grow in grace, as Believers. It is our responsibility to spiritually grow, and you have commanded us to. Lord, my desire is to do what you've called and commanded us; to grow in grace, to increase our understanding of you and to develop a close and intimate relationship with you; when you said in 2 Peter 3:18, KJV: "But grow in the grace and knowledge of our Lord and Savior Jesus Christ. To him be glory both now and forever! Amen" Thank you Father for your written word, which helps me - as many, to understand your Word of Truth. And, thank you for the indwelling Holy Spirit, who has promised and is presently, guiding me in the way that I should go. I pray that I may continue to learn and walk faithfully in spirit and truth. I pray I may come to know you and not just of you more and more each day. This is my prayer and my desire, Lord. Amen"

Unfortunately, in this world, there will be controversy and confusion. Conflict is a way of life; and it's inevitable that some of us are constantly indulged in drama and confusion. Yes, some of our own making and some not. Is it because of our disobedience to God? Umm...

Anything confusing is not of God. 1 Corinthians 14:33, KJV tells us: "For God is not the author of confusion, but of peace..." Remember, as Believers, anything we do should be done decently and in order (1 Corinthians 14:40, KJV). We shouldn't allow the drama in our lives and of the world consume or overtake us. Why? We're trusting in Jesus. Besides, God is not a God of turmoil, or confusion; He is a God of order and a God of peace. Is anyone in the midst of confusion? If so, remember 1 Peter 5:7 (KJV), "Casting all your care upon him; for He careth for you."

Is my/your ministry alive and well to the satisfaction of God? Here's a shout-out to all Pastors, Evangelists, Teachers, Prophets, Preachers and Ambassadors for Christ; how's your ministry? Matthew 28:19–20 ESV says: "Go therefore and make disciples of all nations, baptizing them in the name of the Father and of the Son and of the Holy Spirit, teaching them to observe all that I have commanded you. And behold, I am with you always, to the end of the age." Thank God we have the HELPER (John 14:26, KJV). This is a Promise (God's Promise) of an Ally in the conflict with the world. What an Ally! (The Holy Spirit)

I've grown to learn that change is very difficult. Whether it's changing a habit, attitude, job or city, it's always a challenge. There are moments in our lives when a Change is necessary or due. If we take a moment and look within ourselves and see many things about ourselves that we need to Change; we would. Prior to accepting Christ, I assume we all wanted and prayed for Change; and to become what God would have us to be; to be born again and become a New Creature. If I've written, said, or done anything to anyone, or offended anybody - (past or Present), please forgive me. No, nothing has been said or done that's caused me to bring this up – No, I'm just Changed! Changed from the inside out! No, "God is not finished with me yet, in my walk, or in this new way of life." I'm surely not the man I clearly want to be; but thank God, I'm not the man I used to be. NO! I'm not where I want to be or should be - in Him. Still working on loving my brothers and sisters (thy neighbor) as thyself, loving my enemies as God loves me. Realizing we're all works in progress; but me personally, I am a perpetual work-in-progress and every day I'm leaning on Jesus. I thank God that I'm working my way back to Him. Yes, ♪♫"I Miss My Time With Him" And yes, I must continue to be more humbled before Him; and more so, that I've now learned to lift up the name of Jesus. Someone Very Special to me preached a sermon that there's "No Shame in the Name" (Jesus). No, I'm not ashamed and I pray He's not ashamed of me. Oh Yes, I'm "Studying to shew thyself approved unto God, a workman that needeth not to be ashamed, rightly dividing the word of truth" (2 Timothy 2:15, KJV). Yes, I'm also "Growing in Grace and in the Knowledge of our Savior and our Lord Jesus Christ" (2 Peter 3:18, KJV). More often, I'm beginning to allow God to ♪♫"Order My Steps," while learning how to pray, forgive, and be forgiven; how to give of my time to help others; how to Tithe, and to give Offerings unselfishly. I'm also learning how not to quench or grieve the Holy Spirit but allowing Him to lead and counsel me daily. Lastly and definitely, I'm still learning how to resist the devil (Satan) and submit to Christ. By God's Grace, I Shall Overcome! Together, as a Family, ♪♪♫"We Shall Overcome!" I thank God that I am **"Learning the Way, the Truth, and the Life.**" Is there anyone or anybody reading this feel me? Is anybody out there with me? ♪♪♫"A Change, A Wonderful Change Has Come Over Me!" This is My Testimony! Maybe Yours Too! "I Love You Family and Nothing You Can Do About It!" Hallelujah!

BE ENCOURAGED!

EVERY NOW AND then, we all need some encouragement. So, here's a little something' something' to carry you through your week. First, I implore you to read Isaiah 59:19-21 (KJV & NIV); and thereafter, you will know without a doubt that God has your back! Upon reading this particular message, I'd like to leave you with an uplifting thought: Satan may frighten you but he cannot harm or hurt you; because as a Child of God, we are in His omnipotent grip! We're reminded in 2 Corinthians 4:8-9 (RSV) that: "We are afflicted in every way, but not crushed; perplexed, but not driven to despair; persecuted, but not forsaken; struck down, but not destroyed!" Also, in Isaiah 41:10 (RSV), God tells us to: "Fear thou not; for I am with thee: be not dismayed; for I am thy God: I will strengthen thee; yea, I will help thee; yea, I will uphold thee with the right hand of my righteousness." Lastly, I'm comforted to know that the psalmist David, in Psalm 3:3, NIV writes: "But you, Lord, are a shield around me, my glory, the one who lifts my head high." My brothers and sisters, don't fret or be distressed, God "Has Your Back…!" He Got You! Hallelujah! Dropping the Mic🎤...

I'm praying that some, if not most of the Spiritual Messages you're reading encourage, touch and uplift each of you in a miraculous Spiritual way. I know that each message blesses each individual differently, considering each situational differences and circumstances. Now I'd like to take this opportunity to share one more message within a message that hasn't changed and deserves repeating, even now; and that is: "God Loves You and So Do I"! Several Times I've been made aware that when read, these Spiritual Messages are a blessing (Thank You Lord); so, I'm praying and asking God to bless all readers accordingly - His way, His time; and while or however you're being blessed, please be a blessing to someone else. Enjoy your readings and be encouraged. To God be the Glory!

How Can We Not (**HCWN**) praise, HCWN shout with joy, (**HCWN**) sing praises, (**HCWN**) testify? BUT GOD! (**HCWN**) worship and/or glorify Him? BUT GOD! (**HCWN**) be the Kingdom man or Kingdom woman He knows we can be? BUT GOD! (**HCWN**) be in Him and allow Him to be in us? BUT GOD! (**HCWN**) love Him and show Him? BUT GOD!!! **How Can We Not?**

Some of us have been told to "Let go and let God!" For us to allow God to take control, we have to put our cares, our problems, our circumstances in His hands. For us to let Him have His way, we must have faith… trusting Him to do so. Yes, it's our situation, but His will. "Father, if you are willing, take this cup from me; yet not my will, but yours be done" (Luke 22:42, KJV). C'mon yawl, "Let God!" Just Let Him. He's Able…

There are times in our lives when we need Resuscitation; maybe we need to be Rebooted, a Restart, Refreshed; or, just maybe a good old fashioned Revival? A **Jesus** Revival! There is no other name given to men, that we can be saved. Oh this precious name can take a life and start it all over again. That name is JESUS. Ask, and ye shall receive. ♪♫"Revive us oh Lord, Revive us…" Have Mercy!

When you enter a dark room and turn on the light, the darkness has no choice but to flee. Darkness cannot exist in the presence of light. If you ever find yourself in a dark place, within this dark world, turn your light on or pray for the never ending light from above. In fact, we should have that same light within each of us. Yes Lord, Jesus is the Light! He's the Light of the world! I don't know about you but, ♪♫"This little light of mine I'm going to let it shine, let it shine, let it shine." ♪♫"Jesus, The Light of the World!" Hallelujah!

Somebody got up today with a smiling face but a heavy heart. Was it you? Was it me? Often, we go through days with our spiritual eyes closed. Today, let's greet everyone we meet with our spiritual eyes open; and, with a real agape smile. It's the God in you and, you just might be the one that makes their day. Go ahead… I dare you! I'm smiling now, are you?

When we came into the Kingdom of God, not only were we transformed, we were translated from the kingdom of darkness into the glorious Kingdom of God. We were born again into the family of God as His children. And, because we are children of God, we are joint heirs with the Lord Jesus Christ. That means everything is ours because of Him! Anyone feel rich?

Weekly, we prepare ourselves to step out into the day and/or the weekend, never really thinking about what's out there waiting for us or our loved ones here in this society; did we stop and pray? It's important to give God a moment out of our busy lives. Don't leave home without Him. I know there's something He's done for you to thank Him and give Him praise. Just take this moment now to honor, praise, and thank Him. He is so worthy! Hallelujah!!!

Years ago, an NBA basketball player once said he wasn't anybody's hero or role model. Looking back, he was. He didn't know it but he was setting the example then and we as Christians are today. We set the example as followers and believers of Christ. People are watching our walk, talk, our actions and our stand. What are they seeing, when they look at us? What are they seeing, when they look at you? We are examples.

Our God is an almighty God who sits high and looks low, and He knows exactly what each of us are going through. He knows every minute of our pain and suffering. He not only knows what we feel, He also knows why we feel what we feel. He knows how it happened, and how intense it is and how long it's going to last. He knows every emotion associated with it;

and when we are going through such difficult times, all we can do sometimes is pray and say, "Father, You Know!" And, "Father, I stretch my hands to thee, No other help I know"

When something tragic happens in our lives, we ask God the question, "Why?" because it is our natural and carnal response. What we are really asking Him; though, is not so much "Why, God?" as "Why me, God?" or "Why not?" Must Jesus bear the cross alone, and all the world go free? No, there's a cross for everyone, and there's a cross for me. Yes, each of us has a cross to bear. Are we carrying our crosses? Jesus had help, let Him help you!

Recently, I either read or someone inspired me with this analogy of God: God is like a navigation device; we ask God to lead us, Spiritually, God says go left but we took a right. Yes, we got off the path. Thank God, He is a forgiving God. He sees where we are and leads us back on the path to righteousness (back to Him). Remember, when the Holy Spirit says go, go. Now, please, take a moment and think, meditate, and pray about that; and too, read (Proverbs 3:5, KJV)? Yawl Be Blessed!

We all know of iconic and celebrity figures with acronyms like; MLK, JFK, LBJ, SWV and TLC, to name a few. But we don't know them personally. Well, I don't. Some of us, or most of us; and I pray all of us know JC (Jesus Christ). And not just know of Him. All of us should want to personally **Know Him**. He's the one we truly and personally need to have a relationship with. We, can call on Him anytime from anywhere, for anything. Get to **Know Him** and not just of Him. I think I just dropped the mike again! Smile…

Today, this day; is a story of patience, perseverance and faith, because it is every day that we are faced with an unknown tomorrow, uncertain fate and an unsure future. Let us therefore conquer every day with optimism grounded on prayer… They say prayer changes things… (Smile) I'm smiling because I know it does. Who's smiling with me?

Some, if not most of us are truly blessed and highly favored, but we don't always notice it. God sends a word in an answer sometimes before we ask; or even before the test is given. God is a way-maker. So, whatever you ask or whatever your test, look at the words God has already given. The answer just might be looking us right in our face. God always keeps His promise (Joshua 21:45, KJV). And, I'm a witness that in multiple instances, God has made a way out of no way! Oh yes He has. Are there any witnesses?

Yes, faith and prayer are invisible, but they make impossible things possible. It's God's part to do the wonders, ours is the simplest, to trust and pray. Proverbs 3:5-6 (KJV) tells us to, "Trust in the Lord with all thine heart; and lean not unto thine own understanding. In all thy ways acknowledge him, and he shall direct thy paths." Remember, Mark 9:23, KJV says: "all things are possible to him that believeth." Are you a Believer?

The everyday struggles of life's battle do not always favor those who are stronger or faster; the one who truly wins is the one whose heart says, "I can do all things through Christ which strengthens me." These winners also know to, "Trust in the Lord with all thine heart; and lean not unto thine own understanding." And, because of who they are and whose they are, they already know and believe that, "Victory today is mine" Can I get a witness?

There are times when we can feel so isolated and alone. Our personal and circumstantial concerns weigh heavily on our minds and can sometimes turn our thoughts to despair. Know that we are never alone. God is always by our side. It may take Him sometime to work out all things for our good and His glory, but this is so our burden becomes lighter. We should know that He never rests working for us. He's working right now on our (yours and mines) behalf. Let Him work…Let go and let God!

As Believers, we believe that God is working in our lives to use both the good and the bad for a greater purpose - HIS. Nothing that God allows happens to us is a waste. Disappointment turns into hope as we watch God redeem our current adversity, and even our mistakes. Even evil meant against me, God uses it for good. My Good, His purpose! And, His Glory! Yes, God is working in our lives. Again, get out of His way and Let Him Work! Are you a benefactor of His Work? Hallelujah!

"Perceptions!" Daily, we put on our smiles, wear the finest clothes, flash expensive bling, live in the nicest cribs, drive the coolest cars, meet and hang with all the right people, and saying all the right things. Everybody see us at the top and think we got it going on; many even hating and disrespecting. But nobody knows the tears, the heartbreak, and the struggle we endure. But God see us, He knows all and sees all. Yeah, it's the ♪♪"God in me" (Grammy Award-winning Contemporary Female American Gospel Duo, Mary Mary). Let's never Forget God's love for us. Yeah, God's Got Us! Do you have Him?

Trust is important in any relationship. Can God trust You, Me (Us)? Can He trust us as His Ambassadors, His Disciples, or His Apostles? Can He trust us as His Soldiers in His Army? Can He trust us as His Servants? Can He trust us to be His Vessels? What have we done to earn His trust? Yes, He loves us, but can He trust us? First, we must Trust Him. To trust Him, we must accept and follow His Son (Christ). We must obey Him (be obedient) and grow in Him. Then, maybe, He'll trust us; He'll trust us to be and do what He'll have us to be and do, in Him. (Proverbs 3:5-6, KJV) C'mon, 'Try Him and Trust Him'? He's worthy and He's waiting.

At times, we are faced with a desire (the flesh) that no one or nothing can fill. We try all kinds of things to fill it, but to no success. God said: "Come unto me, all ye that labor and are heavy laden…" We are reminded that ONLY GOD, can meet our every need; only, if we let/allow Him. Philippians 4:19 (NIV) says: "And my God will meet all your needs according to the riches of His glory in Christ Jesus." That's why He's my "Jehovah-Jireh" ("The Lord Will Provide") Let Him!

The new life I have is a life lived through Jesus; at the right hand of God, who directs my path. He "Orders My Steps;" yes, I am led by the Holy Spirit. Jesus Christ died for me, and now I live for Him; To Heaven He ascended, my place to prepare. He's preparing a place for us (you and I) a prepared people. John 14:3 (KJV), Jesus said: "And if I go and prepare a place for you, I will come again, and receive you unto myself; that where I am, there ye may be also." Is anyone out there prepared (who's preparing)? Just asking…

Did you know that God has arranged events and placed people in our lives for a reason? In the same way, we have been appointed to be part of someone's life for a reason as well. And yes, maybe someone has been placed in our lives for a reason. Regardless which, we must make that reason count, because for every life we touch, we are gaining treasures for our own. So, let's be a Gift. Jesus was a Gift. Jesus sent a Gift. And yes, Jesus is Love… So, Love your neighbor, our brothers and sisters. Glory!

My Sisters, my Brothers, whatever our hand finds to do, let's do it with our might, for there is no work or thought or knowledge or wisdom in the grave, to which we are inevitably going. Therefore, my beloved family, be steadfast, immovable, always abounding in the work of the Lord, knowing that in the Lord our labor is not in vain in the Lord" (1 Corinthians 15:58). Whatever we do, do heartily, as for the Lord, and not for glory, self or men (Colossians 3:23, KJV). Besides, "I must work the works of him that sent me, while it is day: the night cometh, when no man can work" (John 9:4, KJV). Who's ready to work for the 'Master'? (John 9:4, KJV)…

Don't ever compare yourself with anyone. Be proud of who God made you to be. If He wanted us all to be alike, He would've made us that way. Be yourself, everyone else is taken. God made us individually, in His image and He didn't make any junk or any mistakes. If you just have to be like someone, be like Jesus! ♫♪"To Be Like Jesus…"

Yes, sometimes God pushes us to our limits…He tests us beyond our endurance, because He has greater Faith in us than we have in ourselves! He knows just how much we can bear. Everything in life is temporary because everything changes! That's why it takes great courage to love, knowing it might end anytime. But having the Faith, it will last forever! Have faith in God, His love never fades or ends. Have faith, God has you!

We've all had some good days, we've all had some hills to climb; we've all had some weary days, and oh yes, some sleepless nights; but, when we look around and we think things over, we realize that all of our good days out-weigh our bad days, We Can't Complain. Yes, the Lord has been good to us; so good, more than this old world or anyone living or deceased could ever be. So, let's just take this opportunity to say - Thank You Lord, Thank You Lord, We Can't and We Won't Complain… Hallelujah!

We may not always know where life's road will lead us. But keep moving. Someone is walking with us. Yes, keep running for that Someone Special. You know life is good when somebody remembers (God). Life is uplifting when Someone is always there (Holy Spirit). Life is great when Someone would protect you and suffer you (Jesus). Cherish life because Someone always cares. Thank You Lord/Jesus (That Someone)!

It's a beautiful thing to walk with the Lord when our heart needs company. To take His hand when we feel all alone. To turn to Him when we need a shoulder to lean on. He's the only one we can always rely or count on. The Lord is waiting to give us His grace and His love. Whatever our cross, whatever the pain, God always has a rainbow after the storm and rain. He promised never to leave us nor forsake us. ♪♪♫"Walk With Me Lord…" (Bishop G. E. Patterson).

As we are blessed to move into our new day, or whatever day we're in, remember that God has chosen and allowed us to rise that day, while someone somewhere did not. Take this gift and build on it, Let us serve the Lord, by serving one another. Let Our Light Shine… It's not about me or you (us); it's about JESUS (Him). He is the Gift that keeps on giving. He has physically given us life, thus far. Can you spiritually feel the life in Him; towards receiving eternal life, through Him? It's just a thought. C'mon, pray on it?

If we, who loves Him, proclaim it and say we love Him, should we show everyone (the world) how much we love Him? God has shown us how much He loves us, (John 3:16, KJV). It's our turn… What Shall We Render? Our Life! C'mon, show God, as to the world just how much you love Him. C'mon, "You Can Do It"!

If God is for us, it really does not matter who is against us. Yes, we have weaknesses, but God has strength. We fall, but God picks us up and forgives us. We fail, but God never gives up on us. He never fails! So, enjoy Him and His gifts of peace, love and joy! You know God is our Father, Jesus is our big brother, and the Holy Spirit is our best friend, (our Counselor). What a beautiful Holy Trinity to have a connection with. Are you connected to the Triune?

Has anyone ever been awaken spiritually with questions about pleasing God? Asking yourself, am I where He wants me to be? Is my living in vain? Is my Light shining bright enough to draw those who are in darkness – to Him? Have I studied to show thyself approved unto god? Have I grown and am I still growing in grace? Am I a hearer only and not a doer of His word? Have I donned the whole armor of God? Am I tired, because I've been running for Jesus a long time? Umm…Some serious questions to answer and some important things to think about, while I'm now awake.

Can we start the day off reminding ourselves with these few comments? If you don't trust Him, *get to know Him*; If you don't know Him, *learn of Him*; If you don't believe Him, *ask Him*; If you don't follow Him, *seek Him*; If you don't have Him, *get Him*; If you don't Love Him, *Try Him*. So, where are you with Him (Jesus)? I pray that the answer is: all of the above!

There's a particular song that I'd like to share with yawl and it's been deeply on my mind;

I've been spiritually overwhelmed with it, repeatedly humming and singing it. It's called: ♪♫"I'm Willing," - I'm Willing To Wait on The Lord God Almighty" (The Caravans, 1958). Some of us may or may not be familiar with this song; nevertheless, we all still should be willing to continue to Pray, Trust, Stand and Wait on God. Yes, wait on the Lord. I'm a witness; He'll be right on time. Are you willing? In season and/or out of season, WAIT.

At times I wonder why God do us like He does. Why does God Love us like He love us. Why does He bless us like He does; even when we're not exactly where He wants us to be; are we deserving, probably not! Why does He give us mercy and grace? Maybe, just maybe, we need to show Him we are worthy; that we are grateful, that we love Him! C'mon yawl, We Can Do This?

Some of us, if not most of us have an old favorite gospel song or hymn that we like to sing in adoration or prayer. Today, let's hum (low, steady, continuous sound) and/or lowly sing it over and over... hopefully having words of edification, consolation, or encouragement. Make sure it's one that warms our heart, makes us smile with joy, gets us all teary-eyed, and/or, causes us to get our silent shout on. So, don't be ashamed and don't hesitate! Get Your Hum On! My mother (rest her soul) literally taught me this song: - anyone heard of, ♪♫"Sweet Home"? (The Angelic Gospel Singers) and (Rev. Cleophus Robinson & Josephine James, 1961). Yawl excuse me while I start humming/singing. ♪♫ I'm getting my hum on right now!

There may be a few of us who have a serious testimony, not a testalie of how God has blessed us physically, financially, and especially spiritually. Maybe a few of us, not all, have witnessed God's Grace, Mercy and Omnipotence. And we now know who we are in Christ; and because of Christ, we truly have something to praise, glorify and thank Him for. Teary-eyed, I do. Are any of you? Maybe someone out there feel me... Praises!

A few moments ago, God smiled at me; although, I didn't see Him, I felt Him, I felt His majestic presence. I'm sharing the same courtesy with each of you readers right now by consciously giving you a warm smile and some spiritual love that your heart can feel even without seeing you. Can you feel me? I, just like you are a member of the body of Christ... God is in me and me in Him. He's in you. He's in us!

When God drops obstacles (stumbling blocks) along our path in life, although we try, don't avoid them, deal with them. They were designed to teach us to be stronger, for His Glory, to test our faith... God always has a reason for allowing things to happen. We may never understand His wisdom but we simply have to trust His will. Proverbs 3:5 KJV says: "Trust in the LORD with all thine heart; and lean not unto thine own understanding." I will trust Him, will you?

In 1967 a song was released by an English rock band called The Beatles said: ♪♫"I get by with a little help from my friends" Well, with that in mind, "All of my help comes from the Lord." He's my friend. ♪♪"I can depend on God through the storm, through the rain, through sickness and through the pain. Yes I can…" I know for sure that: ♪♪"There's not a Friend like the lowly Jesus. No, Not One! No, Not One!" ♪♪"He's a friend that sticketh closer than a brother." And, "Oh what a friend we have in Jesus." Yes, He's my best friend forever (My BFF), is He yours?

Do any of us remember the first time we met God. Do any of us remember our first personal introduction to Jesus? Of course, everyone's experience is different. It's a blessing that we know; God met us where we were, as we were and the way we were. We came as we were… He welcomed us; into Him, as a member of the Body. Are we aware that Jesus is our source, from which all blessings flow? "Don't Miss Your Blessings!" ♪♪"Come to Jesus, Come to Jesus, Come to Jesus just now" (Mahalia Jackson, 1971).

Sometimes, and every now and then, we (awake) get up and head out into some heavy situations. Did we pray about it? Did we remember any of the Lord's promises? Remember, the Lord reminded us that we are not alone, that He'd never leave us or forsake us. When did He ever lie to you? No one knows what each new day brings. Times do get rough; but dig in, stand, trust, believe, and know that God is with you!

I'm a Happy Camper! Why? I'm feeling full of Spiritual Joy. You too? I have JOY that the world didn't give me and the world can't take it away. I am not ashamed to tell you Jesus is the Center of My Joy. All I know that is good and perfect comes from Him. I am full of JOY because of whom He is in me and who I am in Him. If only I had the time to tell yawl about ♪♪"This Joy That, I Have…" Maybe, some of you know what I'm talking about and how I truly feel. Maybe?

There will be times in our lives when God seems distant; when the darkness of disasters hit and there appears to be no end to the heartache and the pain. When these times come, I know it's easy to say: hang in there, don't any of us dare quit, STAND (on His Word). God sees and knows our heartaches and pains; and, He cares. There may be times we will slip, maybe even fall, but we must keep the faith and we will see; God will keep His promise and Joy will come in the morning. A reminder; those of us who seem to be going through and in darkness, the Light is on its way. Jesus, He is the Light of the World.

Only in God, we are truly safe and secure. Whether we are surrounded by mighty walls of stone, a comfortable house, lots of so-called friends and associates, or abundant money; truth is, we can never predict what tomorrow may bring. Besides, tomorrow is not promised to anyone. Our relationship with GOD is the only security that cannot be taken away from us. Stay Close to Him. He won't leave you. Is He with you now.

Everyone has history; yes, a past sin we're not proud of. We've tried to bury it, but every now and then that sin resurfaces. It usually shows up when we're upset, discouraged, disappointed, etc.... News Flash!!! God has a plan for each of us. So don't let our past dictate our future. We belong to God; now, let's make your own history with Him. Remember, we are redeemed. Hallelujah!

When God wants to send you a gift, He wraps it up in a problem. Is it a test of faith towards Favor? The bigger the problem He wraps it in, the bigger the gift it contains. Our situation may look impossible, but we should never rule out the favor of God. We may not see how it can happen, but that's not our task. Our task is to TRUST! Trust God, as He trusts us as His faithful servants. How can we acquire God's favor? Our task is to BELIEVE! Believe in God, as He believes in you. Trust and Believe in the Lord Jesus. We can't find Favor no other way. Now, who wants a gift (Favor)?

I am in the Spirit; and existentially - I am, because I exist. I am something, somebody... I am in Him and He's in me. I am who I am, because of Him, "The Great I AM." I am a member of the body of Christ. I am the branch that cannot bear fruit of itself, except I abide in the one who says: "I Am the True Vine... Yes, I am a child of (the King) God. I am grateful to be who I am in Christ, the Great I Am! Who are you and, whose are you? If you're in Him, as I, then you are blessed beyond measure!

We all know about fair weather friends. We also know that friends come and go. Well, let me educate you about my BFF. Yes, I have a BFF (Best Friend Forever) and I'd like to recommend my BFF to you. He's a friend closer than a brother or sister; He keeps all of my secrets; He's always there when you need Him; and, He'll always be one you can trust. If you'd like, you can call Him Lord, Saviour, Teacher, Masters, or just Jesus. I do! And, I'm willing to share Him. If any of you want to meet my BFF, please, don't hesitate to contact me; I'm excited to introduce Him, and I just know He'll be overexcited to meet any of you. Better yet, you can call on Him (Jesus) yourself anytime. Holler?

"Truth We Ignore" We often forget that we can and do anger the Father. Unfortunately, some do so more than others. Lord, I don't want to be in that number. Yet, it is obvious that God wants the best for us, so when we sin it grieves the Father and in many cases even angers Him. It's good to know that our Father is a forgiving, patient, loving Father. Yes, we are His children; so, let's self-check our sins, repent and thank God for His Mercy and Grace. It's okay to get angry, just don't' sin. Amen?

"What then shall we say to these things? If God is for us, who can be against us?" (Romans 8:31 KJV) "God is for us!" Now, who is for us? Jesus' answered: "anyone who extends a helping hand, who shelters the homeless, who cares for the earth, who feeds the hungry, teaches the ignorant, stands for justice, gives a cup of water in my name, is all for us! Who are you for? Who's on the Lord's side??? Feel free to raise your hand – Smile... Remember when nobody else was there for you, God was there and He promised to never leave us nor forsake us. Take time, take this opportunity to be there for someone else and be a blessing. Glory to God!

As each of us travel going about our day, make sure we are not the drivers. In fact, make sure you ask the Lord to drive you (guide you) and keep you (cover you). Let God be the Captain of your ship and the author of your faith. We are His Children and He's our Father! And, if He's your Lord, let Him lead you; yes, be led. (Romans 8:14 KJV) For as many as are led by the Spirit of God, they are the sons of God. By the way, be blessed today and while you're at it, be a Blessing. Someone's waiting on you.

There's an old (1974) song I'm very fond of. It is song by the renowned artist Gladys Knight & The Pips. Now, I don't know who she was referring to in the song: "You're the Best Thing That Ever Happened to Me;" but when I sing it, (yes, I sing –smile). He (Jesus) is "the Best Thing that ever happened to me". My wife is second, (smile).

One of the shortest powerful names I know is GOD. The greatest abundant word I know is BLESS. And the person I wish all the best today is YOU! God Bless You! May God also bless and give you a caring heart so that you can become a whole person, not just gifted with intellect that can understand, but with the knowledge and a heart that truly cares and loves. If you are reading this message, God Bless You!

Is there anyone ready for some Godly moments? Okay: Happy moments, **Praise** God; difficult moments, **Seek** God; busy moments, **Bless** God; quiet moments, **Worship** God; idling moments, **Trust** God; painful moments, **Connect** with God; and, lovely moments, **Thank** God. Christianity is not a theory or speculation, but a way of life; it's also not a philosophy of life, but a living presence. Let us strive to 'Live on Purpose' 'Living for Christ'.

We all are created by an omnipotent, loving, and merciful God. So when another one of God's creation, tries to block or build walls to keep Gods other creations (you and me) from their purpose, God will move. He will move in ways to take us over and/or through. We're all created for a purpose (His). It's not in our time, But Gods… Nothing can separate us from the love of God. Can I get just one witness? I feel like Praising Him!!!

Sometimes struggles are exactly what we need in life. Yes, you and I! If God allows us to go thru life without obstacles, we would not be as strong as what we could have been or claim to be. Agree? We must have faith; faith is the answer. You know God balances our lives by giving us blessings to keep us happy and enough burdens to keep us humble. Remember, if God brings you to it; He will lead you through it. So remember, if God be for us, who can be against us? I'm excited He's for me!

Whenever we get hurt, tired and stressed, just face a mirror and say, "God never created this beautiful creation to be depressed." Besides, we are too blessed to be stressed! Stay blessed yawl. Whatever it takes in Jesus Name, Stay Blessed! In addition, while you're at it, you can be a blessing to some stressed soul. Remember, we all once were lost, but now we are found. We were blind, but now we see. When you look in the mirror, I pray we see Him… because it's not about you, I'm just sayin'…

If people say you are nothing, let them speak what they feel, don't bother with a response. Being nothing does not harm you until your mind and soul agree with it. Have faith in yourself." Live life with a joyful heart, live on purpose, keep your spirit young and free! Stay true and firm to Jesus Christ! Moreover, be the best that you can be. Know that god loves you and so do I. Praises!

I'd like to share with yawl a story about some favorable blessed people; unfortunately, they fell out of God's grace (God's favor). They became slaves to other existing entities, (lust, money, etc…). By the Grace of God, one day these people finally repented of their sins, and they started praying, praising and following God's and Jesus' commandments. God restored them and lifted them higher than ever before. Don't Those People sound familiar? If God be for us, who can stand against us? As I look in a mirror, I see who one of those people were. Are you looking too?

I think it safe to say that we've all been through the storm; or, possibly still going through storms, as we read this spiritual message… We've experienced trials and tribulations. I don't know your story and you don't know mines; but, we all have a story. God Knows… He's brought us through, thus far. Leading us and sometimes carrying us, at our times in need. Thank God, He's with me, in me; and, I'm with Him, and in Him. Hallelujah!

Recently, while watching the News, and reading the Newspaper; I was thinking about our communities, our society, our people our churches, and our government and the turmoil they're in. What happened to peace, love thy neighbor, honor, integrity, morals and values? Our society is in turmoil because of lack of our beliefs. We need to lean on God's guidance. Remember, we e are the salt…, the only ones that can make a difference in our society. God will lead us, only if we allow Him to. Go ahead, I dare you?

While studying scriptures, I was reminded that every day we must die to self. Not our will, but the will of God, through Jesus our lord. The struggle may seem insurmountable on our own, but with Jesus, all things are possible. We can't do anything without Christ and thus, we can do all things through Him who strengthens us. I don't know about you but I feel Strong… "Finally, my brethren, be strong in the Lord, and in the power of his might" (Ephesians 6:10, KJV).

When we are living righteous, pleasing god; did you Know God never closes a door without opening a bigger one? He always gives us something better when He takes something away. Yes, when God closes a door, He opens another one; or, even a window… but at times He shuts both, for our good. God know us and He knows what's best for us. Trust Him, because He Got You! Are you ready to count your blessing?

While reading some select scriptures, I read that we are nothing without the Lord. "For without me ye can do nothing" (John 15:5, KJV). In addition, that we must delight in the Lord; "Delight thyself also in the Lord; and he shall give thee the desires of thine heart" (Psalm 37:4, KJV). We should start and end each day saying, "Lord, I owe you everything, and by your grace I will repay you. Now, let us always delight ourselves in the Lord. How delightful!

No one has traveled the road of success (Salvation) without ever crossing the streets of failures (Sin). God never promised us an easy journey in life, only safe arrival. The Journey to God starts with one small step at a time. Step-by-step, the journey goes on. Little by little it may seem so long. God doesn't expect us to run the mile but He promises to give us the strength to go the distance. The things we learn on the way will keep us on the righteous path (not the religious path). Our faith in God will keep us strong. Remember, be encouraged, be strong in the Lord and in the power of His might; and, always keep the faith! "Order My Steps, Lord?"

In the oceans and seas of life, (though the storms keep on raging in my life) God is our buoyant force. No matter how strong the winds and how gigantic the waves are, we will not sink because we are anchored to Him (Jesus). ♪♪"Yes, my soul has been anchored in the Lord." Life is a matter of perspective, either we complain because roses have thorns or we rejoice because thorns have roses. If we complain, we remain… and if the storms don't cease and if the winds keep on blowing, despite the tides of life, my word to all reading this message is keep your soul: "Stay anchored in the Lord." Remember, "Through the Storm, Jesus is with you to, 'Stay On Course.'"

Jesus Paid It All – All to Him I Owe… When Jesus was carrying His Cross, He despised the shame of it; but He did it for the joy of paying the price for you and I. Jesus suffered great agony to pay your debt and mine. Looking unto Jesus the author and finisher of our faith; who for the joy that was set before Him endured the cross, despising the shame, and is set down at the right hand of the throne of God (Hebrews 12:2, KJV). How are you with carrying your cross? Is it heavy, (Matthew 11:28-30, KJV)?

Agree to disagree, I believe a blind man is not disabled; he is only unable to see with his eyes. Inability is not disability. A person with a blind mind is worse for he/she cannot see a way out of their difficulties and he/she cannot see the opportunities around them; therefore, they suffer. We all face storms that threaten to confuse or disorient us. When we are blinded by life's disappointment, let's not trust our instincts. God wants to guide us (Holy Spirit), and His word is packed with wisdom and insights for living. His word is a lamp to our feet and a light to our path! "I once was blind but now I see…"

"I Have a Dream" is a public s 17 minutes long speech delivered by American Civil Rights Activist Martin Luther King Jr. during the March on Washington, DC, in 1963. I Have a Dream! In Christ, it's not how high we build our dream that makes a difference, but how high our faith can climb. It's not how much we accomplish but how many lives we touch. God has planted a seed of faith in our hearts, so all we had to do was water it with prayers, fertilize it with Gods word and cultivate it with lots of love. I Love the Lord! What's wrong with you? In memory of Dr. Martin Luther King.

Has anyone ever had to search for something and didn't find it? Well, here's something especially for you: Search for truth and you shall find beauty; Search for beauty and you shall find love; Search for love and you shall find God; and, Search for God and you shall have them all! The loveliest day comes when we wake up one morning and discover the truth that love still colors our beautiful world. How beautiful and lovely to be loved by Jesus. Have a Lovely Day!

Because "He Didn't Have to Do it, But He Did," Jesus is the only one we should follow. He came saying, "I am the way, the truth, and the life: no man cometh unto the Father, but by me" (John 14:6, KJV). He also said, "ye shall know the truth, and the truth shall make you free" (John 8:32, KJV). Jesus always served the truth without compromise; and there will be no compromise in the Bride either, not even with friends or loved ones. The Bride will depend on Jesus and know that He is the burden bearer. No, ♪♪"He Didn't Have To Do It."

We all know that mornings are reminders that God loves us! We're not just given another day to enjoy but a chance to right the wrong of yesterday and the days before... Yes, it's a New Day with New Blessings. So, don't let yesterday's failures and mishaps ruin the beauty of today. Blessings of God are new every morning; every day. Yes, this day is the day that the Lord has made; and this day has its own promise of Love, Forgiveness, Joy and Success. This is Your Day! Enjoy!

As God's children, we will be fought and lied about. People lied about Jesus too; and what did He do? He was oppressed, and He was afflicted, yet He opened not his mouth: "He is brought as a lamb to the slaughter, and as a sheep before her shearers is dumb, so He openeth not his mouth" (Isaiah 53:7, KJV). We should not and cannot pay attention to people in what they say or believe; but, we must know in whom we have believed. I'm also reminded in, II Timothy 1:12, KJV, "For I know whom I have believed, and am persuaded that He is able to keep that which I have committed unto Him against that day." Jesus, I believe!

When everything in this world looks dark, it's hard to believe there is any Hope. But Hope is always there, even when we can't see it. As soon as we let go of our fear, and reach for that Hope it will show itself. ♪♪"My hope is built on nothing less than Jesus' blood and righteousness…" Let's keep Hope alive and may Hope remind us daily that God is always with us! Remember, He promised He'd never leave us nor forsake us. Trust Him. I do!

We shouldn't be misinformed or confused, God didn't add another day in our life because we needed it; He added it because someone out there needs us (me, you). Someone needs to see Christ - in YOU! Someone needs to see Christ - in US! Knowing God works in us and through us should make us more, not less, active in the good works He has planned for us. This is not just another day, "This is the day which the LORD has made; we will rejoice and be glad in it" (Psalm 118:24, KJV).

"The Good News" If we proclaim to be a born again, we should be grateful that we are one of the redeemed ones and that we are in debt (a Servant) to the human race through Jesus Christ. We have the truth, and we should never be ashamed of it but be ready to shout it to the world. Scripture in Romans 10:11, (KJV) says: "Whosoever believeth on him shall not be ashamed." We should be so grateful to Jesus for paying our debt of sin that we want to spend our lives telling others the good news. ♪♫"Said I wasn't gonna tell nobody But I, oh I, oh I, I couldn't keep it to myself!"

You may or may not be aware that God did not promise days without pain, laughter without sorrow, or sun without rain. But He did promise strength for the day, comfort for the tears; and a Light for our way. Like the rain can't be stopped from falling, God's love and blessings can't stop; it just keeps on pouring down. I hope you woke up renewed and refreshed and comforted by His Company. I pray you're in His Omniscient Company. This is the day that the Lord has made. We will rejoice, and be glad in it. Rejoice! Rejoice! And be blessed!

God is truly wise. Yes He is! He made sadness so we'd know joy, pain so we'd have pleasure, war so we'd seek peace, hate so we can love and a morning so we can face a new day. God created mornings so that we can say how great the previous day has been and how wonderful the next 24 hours can be! Yes, "This is the day which the Lord hath made; we will rejoice and be glad in it." So, have a blessed day and pray we're all blessed with a beautiful tomorrow. Blessings!

As Pilgrims and strangers traveling through this old barren land; we all travel different paths, prayerfully comforted and guided by the Holy Spirit. We're a part of God's Plan and hopefully, in His Will (thy will be done…) we live to serve Him (but as for me and my house…) For His Glory (to Him be glory and dominion forever…) It's not about me/you/us (yet not I, but Christ liveth in me…). Yes, different paths but the same destination. Together (members of the body), ♪♫"We're marching to Zion…"

This morning I was reminiscing, how good God has been throughout my past; looking back, I saw where I was - compared to where I am currently. Nothing seems to change but it did; I did, and I did not see it happening. I didn't see it coming. I was blind. The struggles, the stress, the hardships, the disappointments, etc.… It was through the trials and even the defeats that God showed up and showed out; and yes, I was revived. I was atoned. I was redeemed! Is God Awesome? ♪♪"Amazing grace, how sweet the sound that saved a wretch like me! I once was lost, but now am found; Was blind, but now I see." Now, "Lord, I thank you for loving me, saving me, choosing and using me that I, as others might be examples of your glory. Amen."

Last night I went to bed with heavy thoughts. This morning, I was awakened with those same thoughts. I was thinking how much I needed someone that I could have a true personal relationship with. Someone who'd be closer than a brother; someone I can talk to; someone I could follow and grow in grace towards becoming like. Who I know would sacrifice His life for me. Someone I could turn to for hope. Someone divine enough to be the center of my joy. Can any of you readers help a brother out? Humbly not wavering… ♪♪"Jesus is the answer…"

As we go through our life journey, like Old Testament Job, God will allow us to be tested, (our faith). We might call it trials and tribulations, but the test isn't about wins and losses; it's about building and refining us. Shaping and molding us… Knowing this, let's stay rooted in the Lord (His Word) and we will be overcomers. We shall overcome some day, if we haven't already. Who's ready to be tested?

None of us knows how our day will start or how it will end. "But as for me and my house, we will serve the Lord." If we all understand the gift of new life we've just been given, realizing we all have a purpose; the question is, are you doing or working on yours? The spiritual premise in a Purpose-Driven Life is that there are no accidents, God planned everything and everyone. He planned for each of us to wake up today; and, for us to read this short spiritual message. Now, what are our plans for Him today?

Often times, we get a spiritual nudge (guided by the Spirit) to physically say or do something. It's likely it will require us to step out of our comfort zone. Remember, God knows what best for us; and we are to be obedient, "Trust in the Lord with all thine heart;…" So, let's pray that each of us grow towards trusting God and for us to be nudged more. Go on, step out on faith. The Holy Spirt awaits you.

Have you ever created something that you were so proud of that you guarded over it daily? One day, somehow, it got damaged. It was broken and damaged but not beyond repair. How did that make you feel? Think on this… How do you think God felt and still feels about His creation? YOU! (Genesis 1:27, KJV) That's why Jesus came (John 3:16, KJV); to sacrifice His life for you, and me. Just a thought… I'm repairable, are you?

Looking in the mirror this morning, rhetorically, I asked myself – Am I living right? Am I serving right? Am I praying right? Am I praising right? Am I worshipping right? Am I loving right? I'm praying that God continue blessing me to be RIGHTEOUS. I certainly don't want to be religious. And, I don't want to be just a churchgoer because I am the Church. "Let the redeemed of the Lord say so..." (Psalm 107:2, KJV)

If any of us had one question to ask the Lord I'd assume it would differ in many aspects; of course, directed towards our salvation. If I may, I would ask the Lord to Endow Me. (Endow: provide with a quality, ability, or asset or a gift) Lord, Endow Me To Speak and Understand Your Holy Word, To Prophecy With Edification, To Cast Out Devils Like Jesus Said, To Heal The Sick and To Speak With Tongues and Give Interpretation. Please, Endow Me. Endow Me Lord. Endow me with the Power of the Holy Ghost. Anyone out there wants to be endowed? I'm just asking...

When we look back and wonder how we ever made it through, how we got over. We realize it's not because we've been clever but because God has been wise; not because we've been strong but because God has been mighty; not because we've been consistent but because God has been faithful. There's only one word to describe it, GRACE. His Grace is sufficient! "Grace in the New Testament is in some respects one of its greatest words. It always means two things - God's Favor and His Blessing; His Attitude and His Action." Now, that's how we made it through! "That's how I got over!"

There are choices within everyone's command. Each of us has our own choices to make. No one has to do, or is obligated to live their lives as others live. On the other hand, inevitably at some point in our lives, we witness, first-hand, choices that others (friends, family members or colleagues) make that we can clearly see are leading them down a slippery slope to either immediate devastation of consequences, or a future that can be potentially harmful. I don't know about yawl, but I've decided to make Jesus my choice. Follow Christ!

Be strong. Never tell yourself, "I'm tired". The more you accept that thought, the more exhausted you'll become. But if you tell yourself, "I can do even more." You'll find that there are no limits to what you can accomplish... for God never gets tired of guiding you all the time. God made you a promise that you won't have to face life alone. For when you grow weak in your struggles, His strength will prevail and not your own. Remember, "I can do all things through Christ..." (Philippians 4:13, KJV)

Here's some Spiritual Food For Thought: Don't work too hard to give yourself the best of everything, instead make a greater effort to give God the best of yourself. If you keep God inside your heart, there is nothing that will come into your life that you won't be able to handle. If you have a problem, don't say "Hey I have a big problem." Rather say, "Hey problem, I have a Great GOD." ♪♪"Praise God from Whom All Blessings Flow."

If you were a loyal best friend and you were always available when problems arose; you knew all the bad dirt that was ever done, all the bad things said, and still, you remain a loving loyal dependable friend to him/her. Through it all, - the mess, you remain loyal. Isn't it something how Jesus has been there for us, through all our mess; and still, remain loyal and He's with us today? "I'm Just Sayin'" "A man that hath friends must shew himself friendly: and there is a friend that sticketh closer than a brother." JESUS!

God is good, all the time; and, All the time, God is Good. God has done much for us. He gave His Son; He forgives us of our sins; He's promised and given us life, peace, and good health. When I turn to Him, He's always there. He may not have come when I wanted Him to, but when He did, He was always on time. So, He's done so much for us, with us, and through us; what can we render to Him? Me, Myself, and I! What Shall I Render to God, MY LIFE? Has He done anything for you lately?

I am thine O Lord and I am here, Master, can you use me? Daily, we are faced with many questions like: Are my Fruits (of the Spirit) ripe and ready to share? Have I done all I need to do so God can use me? Is there something I need to do a little more work on? Am I ready to ask God to SEND ME? Am I wearing the Whole Armor of God, ready for war? Have I surrendered all? If I can unequivocally answer these questions, after being chosen, shaped and molded (as a servant), then and only then I may be ready to ask: "Master, Can You Use Me" Who's ready to ASK? We are blessed to bless others… We serve God through serving one another. I'm ready to be asked, are you?

We are debtors - not to the flesh (world), and not to live according to the flesh (world). For if we live according to the flesh/world we will die; but if by the Spirit, we put to death the deeds of the body/flesh; thus, we will live. For as many as are led by the Spirit of God, these are sons of God. In this realm (world) that we are in, we are being encouraged not to live according to the dictates of our flesh (world), for to do so mean death - separation from God. Romans 8:6, KJV remind us to be spiritually minded to focus on the things of the spirit that brings us life and peace. Let us focus!

Do we really believe Jesus is the Resurrection and the Life; that we should love our brothers and sisters, as He love us? Do we truly believe that??? If you do, then call someone today that you have not spoken with in months or years and just say hello, I miss you. Or, hello, I love you. We may or may know what will happen, but God is alive and moving. C'mon, let Him move through you? Where's your cell phone?

There are times we find ourselves caught up looking at the why's of our situations instead of praying through them; taking them to the Alter. Others are living successful lives, while we are struggling in ours. God reminds us to stay focused on Jesus; hold on to our faith, don't give up – and know that Jesus already got your plan working just for you. Just wait on Him and trust Him. He Got You!

I believe this is a special extraordinary day; why, because God allowed us to be in it. He has allowed you to read this message. Today, many of us might have some difficult moments, but remember those previous struggles? God was with us. We are not alone. He's also with us now. We must fight for our hope and faith. Whatever it looks or feels like; yes, Gods got us. He's got everything we need and everything we want. So, be blessed and while you're at it, be a blessing. Someone out there needs one.

Waking up every morning has become an ordinary part of our lives. But in fact, it's not ordinary at all… It's the first wonderful blessing that we receive every day. So let's thank Him for waking us this morning; whereas, many did not. "Father God we thank you for waking us up, allowing us to walk, talk, and see (to read this wonderful message). Thank you Father for this opportunity for me to be all you would have me to be in you. Amen."

There will always be people who doubt that you are more than what they think – what they think you should be. We're to be careful to who we listen to and start listening to God's label for us. He is the Ultimate Designer. His labels: **CHOSEN, PRECIOUS, FAVORED,** and **BLESSED.** Know that you are made for more! More in Him…Be blessed and keep your ears open for the Shepherd's voice. You just might here "**Child of God**!"

This is the day that the Lord has made. Rejoicing, we've decided to press forward, charge the hill and not settle for whatever. We are more than conquerors! Besides, we can do all things through Christ, which strengthened us. We cannot do this without God. So, praise Him and seek His counsel. So Rejoice, we already have the victory - Hallelujah!

Does any of yawl know that Grace is AMAZING? His grace is not only Amazing, it is 'sufficient'. It is enough! Yes, it's so Amazing! ♪♪♫"Amazing Grace, How sweet the sound - That saved a wretch like me; I once was lost, But now I'm found - Was blind, but now, I see." Let me also share that: ♪♪♫"Amazing Grace shall always be my song of praise For it was grace that brought me liberty. I do not know just why He ever came to love me so; He looked beyond my faults and saw my need." Amazing Grace!!!

I AM REDEEMED

WHO'S REDEEMED? PSALM 107:2, NKJV says: "Let the redeemed of the LORD say so, Whom He has redeemed from the hand of the enemy…" It's a blessing that some, if not most of us are Redeemed Sinners. Are we free from sin? NO! Can we be tempted? YES! Every Christian Believer no matter how spiritual or no matter how long we've been saved; can be and/or will be tempted; just keep on living…

Although it's our nature, do we desire to sin? NO! Are we tempted of sins? YES! It's inevitable that Satan is on his job; he dangles in front of our eyes, many tempted things and as long as we entertain ourselves of them and feed on them, we're susceptible, obviously, to sin. We should not give in to every sin simply because it comes across our path. Of course, temptation is a very common problem for all of us; and, perhaps, victory over temptation is not so common. Yes, now and then, some, if not most of us have fallen short. Romans 3:23, KJV reminds us that, "For all have sinned, and come short of the glory of God."

Once, I was tempted (a short thought of suicide); I Yielded Not. Praise God, I was guided otherwise by the Holy Spirit. Some of us, if not most are tempted daily by many similar and/ or other things. The question is: how much and how many times we yield? Even Jesus was tempted… Sometimes we get into sin, simply because we are tempted. 1 Corinthians 10:13, NIV tells us that God has promised that, "no temptation will be greater than our resistance to bear it; God is faithful…" Being tempted is a Believer's biggest hindrance. Luke 22:40, NKJV says: When he came to the place, he said to them, *"Pray that you may not enter into temptation."*

If we can possibly eliminate temptation, we can eliminate sin. In order for us to be victorious over temptation, we have to put our faith, trust, and focus on Jesus Christ. I am tempted to continue this particular paragraphed message, but The Holy Spirit says end it. I am obedient. ♪♪"Yield not to temptation, for yielding is sin;" Now, I would like to take this opportunity to pray for and with all readers who are presently being tempted at this moment in their lives, in some form or another. Let us pray?

"Father, I ask for your guidance, guide my actions, my thoughts, my words, and my deeds. Lord, you are omniscient; you see it all, my outer circumstances, and my inner turmoil. You made me and you understand my life; how my heart weighs heavy with trouble and misunderstanding. I presently lay all these things before you and please Lord; allow me not to yield to temptation. Lord, right now I seek your encouragement and I ask for your grace, because Hebrews 2:18, NIV says: "For because He himself has suffered when tempted, He is able to help those who are being tempted." And lastly Lord, you said in Joshua 1:9, KJV: "Have not I commanded thee? Be strong and of a good courage; be not afraid, neither be thou dismayed: for the Lord thy God is with thee whithersoever thou goest." Thank You Lord! I'm encouraged. Amen."

SPIRITUAL HEALING

WE ALL HAVE lost someone we dearly love at some time or another. Recently, many of you, have faced a great loss in your lives; losing a mother, sister, or brother; someone we were very close to and cared deeply about. Someone we always thought would be around, then one day we get the grief-stricken news. Losing a close family member; I, as many wept with sorrow and grief. It's was hard on me; very sad, and very hurtful. A painful experience, even though assured that our loved one is in a better place. Upon hearing, like many, I initially felt numb and disoriented, silently crying and hurting deep inside, empathized, I was triggered by memories or reminders of my loved one. Those memories… Yes, grief inevitably strikes us, but by God's grace, sorrow does not have to overcome us. Jesus Himself wept over the death of his friend Lazarus (John 11:35, KJV).

As I prayerfully reflect on my family member's passing, as many other siblings have, I was lead to John 17:24, KJV. You know Christians meet this reality more than most because we belong to a bigger family; we are a Church Family. God is sovereign over our loved ones' deaths, and He has purposes we may never understand (Deuteronomy 32:39; James 4:15, KJVs). The death of a dear loved one may present one of the greatest tests of our faith. But can we trust that our loved one is better off with the Beloved? If we do, then our grief is a Godly Grief, and Jesus will turn our sorrow into great joy (John 16:20, KJV). Right about now, I need joy and I need comforting. What about you? Let us not forget and remember that God is ultimately the source of our comfort (2 Corinthians 7:6-7, KJV).

Let's also remember our passed loved ones' love and the influence they've shared in our lives. We bring our prayers to God asking Him for comfort and healing. God is the Father of mercies (unmerited mercies) and He will comfort us in all our tribulations (2 Corinthians 1:3-4, KJV). Be assured that God loves us and He understands how much we are hurting. Just know when a loved one passes; Jesus gains a lot more than we have lost. Yes, we have loved and we've lost; and we may never again share love and fellowship with that loved one again in this life. If only we could change the past, if only we could alter the circumstances that resulted in our instant loss and constant pain.

Unfortunately, we cannot change the painful past or bring back our loved one; nevertheless, we can live with gratitude for the love we had and for the life we shared. So, we do grieve our losses; nevertheless, life must go on in Jesus Name.

In summation, I believe that our tears and our pain over our losses are exceeded by God's tears and God's pain over our loss. God knows, for God has been there where I am and where many of us have been in our loss. Tragedy can drive us away from God in bitter disappointment or tragedy can lead us to God, closer to Him in longing hope. The choice is ours! During bereavement, I'm comforted by the Holy Spirit; I'm led to God, and I've made Jesus My Choice. I dedicate this Spiritual Message to all who have lost a family member, a friend, or a loved one. They are *"Gone But Not Forgotten"* No, they will never be gone from our hearts! May they "Rest in Peace" and may God be with us all...

REJOICE!

ONE OF THE shortest powerful names I know is GOD. The greatest abundant word I know is BLESS, and the person I wish all the best is YOU! GOD Bless YOU! May God bless and give you a caring heart so that you can become a whole person, not just gifted with intellect that can understand, but with the knowledge and a heart that truly cares and loves so that you may express it in your service. Be blessed family, and while you're being blessed, be a blessing to someone. So, let's Rejoice!

This is a day that the Lord has made - Let's Rejoice!!! Let us acknowledge that God has done much for us in the saving of our lives by sending his own Son as our redeemer and sin-bearer. To serve God is not a grievous or hard task because God is our MASTER, a Great Boss, and a Great Rewarder. In fact the Bible reveals to us that there are great benefits in serving God. Take time to read Exodus 23:25-28, KJV... Also, scriptures say: "If they obey and serve Him, they shall spend their days in prosperity, and their years in pleasures" (Job 36:11, NIV). Now that sounds good to me! So get Yawl's serve on, get your benefits and be blessed. The Lord has made this day, so let us rejoice in it. Rejoice!

Yes! "This is the day the Lord has made; we will rejoice and be glad in it." No matter the circumstance, we should rejoice this Lord's Day and Be Glad In it! Now, can someone please tell me, does it really matter (to Christ) what denomination you/we are? I'd truly love to be in the denomination that Christ is more involved in, that Christ is more attentive to; or, Christ is more favorable to. I would like to be a devout member of a local church where everyone is Sanctified, Holy, and where it does not matter in baptism if we're Sprinkled, Sprayed, or Submerged; or, if we wash feet or not. Can any of us imagine the perfect church or denomination? I'm elated to know that we all can agree on the Father, Son, and The Holy Ghost. We all believe in John 3:16. We all know and accept Jesus as our Savior. I'm praying most of us accept Him as our Lord. We (You and I) are the Church - striving to be perfect in Christ Jesus. We are the body of Christ, the Church of the Living God! (1 Corinthians 12:27, KJV)... And, that's all that matters or is important, anything else is nonessential. So, Be the Church! We are Members of the Body of Christ - with Him as our Head of the Church. I'm with Him. Who You Wit? Now, in the name of the Father, Son and Holy Spirit, Rejoice! Rejoice! Rejoice!

When everything looks dark, it's hard to believe there is any Hope. But Hope is always there, even when you can't see it. As soon as you let go of your fear, and reach for that Hope, it will show itself. May Hope remind us that God is always with us! Remember, He promised He'd never leave us nor forsake us. Trust Him. I do! First, let us "Rejoice," be safe, be prosperous and "Keep Hope Alive!" REJOICE!

Those of us who have been blessed with the Favor of God, Rejoice! Because, "It Ain't Nothin' But A G-Thang Family" The countless Blessings we receive, the Grace and Mercy we receive, "It Ain't Nothin' But A G-Thang Family" The Service that we joyfully and lovingly render to the least of those, "It Ain't Nothin' But A G-Thang Family" The prayers that we pray for healing and deliverance, "It Ain't Nothin' But A G-Thang Family" The prayers that we uplift, on behalf of others, and also, standing in the gap, "It Ain't Nothin' But A G-Thang Family" Those prayers of worship, adoration, and reverence for God and His word, "It Ain't Nothin' But A G-Thang Family" The love for us that God gave His son as a living sacrifice and the love that we have for Him and the obedience to the Holy Spirit, It Ain't Nothin' But A G-Thang Family" F.Y.I., "It Ain't Nothin' But A God Thang Family" and that's all it is! Are you with it? I don't know about you but I'm All In. God is doing HIS THANG in Me, With Me, To Me, and Through Me! C'mon, rejoice! Because, ♪♫"It Ain't Nothin' but a GOD-Thang Family"- ♪♫ "To God Be The Glory..."

I am rejoicing and celebrating praises for being strong in the Lord and in the power of His might and for another opportunity to be led by the Holy Spirit. Sometime ago, I was hospitalized (heart illness); in the great Dorn VA Medical Center in Columbia, South Carolina. I send sincere love and thanks to the Doctors and RN Nursing Staff - via Dr. Jesus who governed over the surgical procedures. I also thank everyone for their prayers, thoughts of kindness and their show of love and support. I was in awe of my permanent visitor, the Holy Spirit who just wouldn't leave my bedside. Who comforted me spiritually, emotionally, and physically every moment, as He is now while I'm writing this message. As I thank each of you, I thank the Holy Spirit, who has also led and allowed me to share my feelings. No doubt, I thank God for a speedy recovery in His time. Meanwhile, being led and being obedient to the Holy Spirit is essential to my salvation, I am grateful. Now, let me also take this opportunity to give a "Shout-Out" to my daily Morning Prayer Warriors. Go, Prayer Warriors, Go!!! May God bless you all...? Rejoicing in God's Hands...

Like many, I am so blessed to celebrate another birthday (October 27th); and I am going to do all I can to stay trouble-free (smile), by allowing the Holy Spirit to guide me. Yes, I'm having a P A R T Y; ♪♫"It'll be My Party and I'll "Shout if I Won't To!" Sorry 'Smokey Robinson' I won't be "The Life of The Party" because Jesus will be. Yes, Jesus, He is the Life (John 14:6, KJV)! Now, excuse me while I 'Get This Party Started' with my beloved wife, my children, and a Few of my friends (The Divine Trinity). We will be celebrating my (Earthly) first Date-of-Birth along with my second Born Again Birthday! Thanks Kool and the Gang... ♪♪"Celebrate good times, come on! (Rejoice, and Let's celebrate)"♪ Now, that's something to Shout and Rejoice about!

I know that some of us, if not all of us go through hard times, having trials and tribulations. Yes, it's rough sometimes. We may ask ourselves, is there any light at the end of the tunnel? Even now, some, most, or all of us are facing complications, hardships and hard times. Do we cry, whine, pout, or throw in the towel? NO! We don't quit, no matter how dire it gets. And we don't have a pity party, protest, or express dissatisfaction. God is still on the Throne. He's still in control. Jesus didn't quit on us. No He didn't'! So, I don't know about yawl but I can't complain. "I Won't Complain;" not now, not ever. I thought I heard someone say: If God doesn't do anything else for me, ♪♪"He's Done Enough" (Beverly Crawford). Hallelujah! Yes, God is Good! So, Who's Complaining?

> ♪♪"I've had some good days, I've had some hills to climb
> I've had some weary days And some sleepless nights
> But when I look around And I think things over
> All of my good days Out-weigh my bad days"
> "I WON'T COMPLAIN"♪ (Rev. James Cleveland)

Trouble! "When it rain, it pours." Life can go on smoothly for a while; things are going great, and then all of sudden Bang! Things go wrong; not just one thing, but several things at once, and we wonder what hit us. It could be a live Christmas tree that won't act right after it's erected (mine); a heating unit that has quit working during winter, a car just broke down on the road, a death in your family, or an unexpected financial expense. "When it rains, it pours". Cartoon fame Charlie Brown once said, "It always looks darkest just before it gets totally black!" Meaning, just when we think things are at their worst...they get really bad. Before we can put one problem to rest, we find ourselves assaulted or bombarded by another - then another...

Unfortunately, we know things don't always go as planned. The truth is, no one sails through life without storms (troubles); we all go through storms, it's something we all have to live and deal with (1 Peter 1:6, KJV). It's a part of our life and we cannot avoid it. As it comes at us and upon us, it brings good and bad, the joy and the pain, the rain as well as the sunshine. We must embrace our trials and our tribulations in order to grow and become Righteous. Scriptures informs us that it rains on the just, as well as on the unjust (Matthew 5:45, KJV). It's important how we respond when the storms come? In the midst of a storm,

I submit to yawl these words, "don't give up when it/they (storm) come or overwhelms you." Thank God, ♪♪♪"Trouble Don't Last Always;" and, isn't it good to also know when trouble rise, because "Weeping may endure for a night, but joy comes in the morning" (Psalm 30:5, KJV)! I'm grateful that when "Trouble in my way, I have to cry sometimes." But, I know that ♪♪♪"Jesus Will Fix It!" Family, we all want to be 'Trouble-Free' but we're counting on Jesus to cover us.

THE HOLY SPIRIT

SINCE GOD IS Spirit, I assume we all are looking for guidance on how to grow spiritually. On how to be endowed by the power of the Holy Spirit, how to be filled with the Holy Spirit, how to be baptized in the Holy Spirit, how to receive the anointing of the Holy Spirit; and/or, how to be led by the Holy Spirit - daily. The Holy Spirit is a Gift... Who doesn't like presents? (Acts 2:38, KJV) As believers, we must praise, worship and be led by the Holy Spirit – our Helper.

Someone somewhere needs a lawyer, a mediator to plead their case. Scriptures says "For there is one God and one mediator between God and mankind, the man Christ Jesus" (1 Timothy 2:5, KJV). Yes, Jesus our Heavenly Advocate will plead our case. So if we sin, we can go to our (mediator) Advocate. He will forgive us, cleanse us and plead our case. "For all have sinned and fallen short of the glory of God (Romans 3:23, KJV). So, Order in the Court!!! Let's All (rise) STAND for God our Judge, Court is in Session... Okay, we're in court; with Jesus as our Advocate. Since we are redeemed, I believe we now need a Counselor (The Holy Spirit).

Do any of you think that someone would comment that: "These Spiritual Messages are too long for me to read." or, "Sometimes I just don't have the time to read." or, "I'm very busy with a lot on my mind." or, "I'm too tired to read anything." or, "Do there have to be so many?" or, "These messages seems to step on my toes and I hate it." or, "I don't think we need to read a Spiritual Message every day." or, "Please, give me a break with those Spiritual messages." or, "Whenever I do read them, I don't have the time to look up the scriptures." or, "I don't need to be Spiritually uplifted every day." or, "These Spiritual Messages are only for those babes in Christ not me." or, "Do they have to be so deep and spiritual" or, "I'll read them whenever I have or got the time which is limited." or, "I don't need to read them because I'm saved." or, "I don't like to read." And so on... It's important for us to see and appraise things with their true value, with the eyes of Christ. When we pray, we do not pray that God will spare us the hard work of rigorous spiritual reading and reflection. Ignoring spiritual uplifting can be one's greatest folly. God's Word is "Spiritually Discerned." With that said, let us strive to be spiritually discerned. And let us also strive to be spiritually mature. I'm a strong advocate for Spiritual Growth. No one should be forced to grow in Christ. It's our choice. I'm just a servant and I thank all of you for reading these Spiritual Messages! They are blessed and ordained by the Holy Spirit. Read, and let the Holy Spirit empower you with knowledge, wisdom and understanding. To God be the Glory!

Thank you Lord. With compassion, we owe you for giving us the Holy Ghost; and outside of salvation, that is one of the greatest gifts He could have given us. "And I will pray the Father, and he shall give you another Comforter, that he may abide with you forever" (John 14:16, KJV). God never sent a greater package down from Heaven, and yet some of us don't look at it that way. Some are even ashamed of the Holy Ghost; but Jesus said, "Whosoever therefore shall be ashamed of me and of my words in this adulterous and sinful generation; of him also shall the Son of man be ashamed, when He cometh in the glory of His Father with the holy angels" (Mark 8:38, KJV). My prayer is that all reading this message receive The "Baptism of the Spirit" (Holy Ghost) (being filled with the Holy Spirit) or being equipped or empowered by God's Spirit to carry out the task that Jesus has given us as 'The Church'. I'm in debt, are you?

Many of us, if not most proclaim that we are Born Again, Saved, and that Jesus is our Savior; and also, our Lord. We say that we KNOW HIM. Not just of Him. So, if we truly and unequivocally Know Him (the Son), then we Know the Father and we also Know (and are led by) The Holy Spirit. This is no game...This is real! God is real! Our Salvation is real! Personally knowing Him is essential. Eternal Life is a Serious Matter! Ask yourself, does my life exhibit the Trinity? Let's get right with God and do it now!!!

Lately, I've been having a healthy conversation with the Holy Spirit about spiritual maturity. As I listened and was counseled (taught), that Christianity and Discipleship is a living, life-long process towards what one might call sanctification which is a process of becoming Holy. It's a gift given through the power of God. The gift of sanctification means to be set apart; you become a peculiar person, different than you were, a new creature, born again; maturing in God's Will, in His Word, and in Christ Jesus. It doesn't mean for you to be holier-than-thou; that you've arrived... No! Me, I'm not there yet. I'm still climbing 'Jacobs Ladder.' Still working in the vineyards towards acquiring God's Gift of sanctity. Personally, I would hope I'm maturing, that I'm growing in grace (2 Peter 3:18, KJV) - but have I arrived? Have any of us arrived? Condescendingly some congregants, but not some of us and not necessarily apostles, prophets, evangelists, pastors or ("shepherds") and teachers (Ephesians 4:11, KJV) strut our biblical knowledge like it was an accomplishment; like we know it all, we got it going on... "We've arrived." But it's not about us and it's never been about what we know or don't know, or, how much we know; but about what God knows, who God is and His love for us through His son. It's about our love for Him and each other, our neighbor. Paul tells us in 1 Corinthians 8:1: "*Knowledge puffs up, but love builds up.*" If we are sashaying our maturity, it's pretty clear we've got some growing in grace (maturity) to do. We're not building and where's the Love? Any one of us can lack spiritual maturity. GROW! Now rhetorically ask yourselves,

"Am I lacking spiritual maturity? Have I arrived spiritually? Am I where I need to be in Christ? Where's my Gift, my Sanctity, and do I sound Peculiar?

I've been trying to find my way to be empowered by the Holy Spirit. I have sought the Lord much to have understanding of the Holy Spirit. I didn't know until now that we can learn so much by being quiet in His (Holy Spirit) presence? So now, scripturally, as in 1 Thessalonians 4:11 (KJV), I study to be quiet… I've heard that the Holy Spirit is a life compass. I've experienced that GOD is so perfect in His directions, so absolute in His decisions, that if we follow Him every step of the way, we have nothing to worry about; and, we will be led… You know, I once was lost but now I'm found. Hallelujah! I'm studying, I'm quiet, and I'm waiting on the Lord to direct me on which way I should go. What about you?

Are we living in a Spiritual Atmosphere? We know that the enemy (Satan) attacks our lives spiritually, if we allow him to. We know there's a physical atmosphere that we can see, smell, hear, and touch; and we also know there's a spiritual atmosphere we cannot see with the natural eye or experience it with the rest of our natural senses, but it is very real. "For we wrestle not against flesh and blood, but against principalities, against powers, against the rulers of the darkness of this world, against spiritual wickedness in high places" (Ephesians 6:12, KJV). We impact our Spirit by the atmosphere we choose. The atmosphere of holiness, purity, praise, worship, prayer, love, and unity attract the Holy Spirit and pleases God; just as an atmosphere of lust, drunkenness, anger, and hatred attracts demonic spirits pleasing Satan. Galatians 5:22-23, KJV says: "When the fruit of the Spirit is in you, you create an atmosphere for the presence of the Holy Spirit." And Ephesians 2:22, KJV says: "He dwells in you. You're a vessel of the Holy Spirit and He will take you into His presence…" If we are filled with the Holy Spirit and He is dominating our lives, He creates an atmosphere for His presence to dwell. So let each of us create an atmosphere of WORSHIP and PRAISE. God manifests His presence when the atmosphere is right. Rhetorically, ask yourselves, "What kind of atmosphere does my life have?" Am I Spiritual or Carnal? Am I Righteous or Unrighteous? What paradigm am I in and/or should be in? Please, be blessed in a Spiritual Atmosphere.

First, let's give honor to our Lord and Savior… It's a blessing to be endowed with the power of the Holy Spirit. When we ask of God for something, we had better know what we are asking and be prepared to receive It; and, run with it. Daily, when meditating, the Holy Spirit empowerment enlightens me and being obedient, I must enlighten someone else. Yes, I'm obligated. I spread the Gospel (The Good News); I must tell the truth and shame the devil. I share what is given me. No, it's not Me/I, but He (Holy Spirit) that's within me! We are all members of the body; are we obedient? Let each of us strive to 'Be endowed', 'Be led' and 'Be blessed' daily in the Lord.

Since God is Spirit, I assume we all are looking for guidance on how to grow spiritually.

On how to be endowed by the power of the Holy Spirit, how to be filled with the Holy Spirit, how to be baptized in the Holy Spirit, how to receive the anointing of the Holy Spirit; and/or, how to be led by the Holy Spirit - daily. The Holy Spirit is a Gift. Who doesn't like presents? (Acts 2:38, KJV) As believers, we must Praise, Worship and be led by the Holy Spirit. Who's being led?

Are we celebrating praises, for being strong in the Lord and in the power of His Might; and. for another opportunity to be led by the Holy Spirit? We all want to grow and know more about the Holy Spirit. Somebody, somewhere and maybe those of us who are reading this message need the Holy Spirit and presently needing a word from the Lord. I would like to impress upon your heart your great need to be filled with the Spirit.

If we live another day without the Holy Spirit's control in our lives, we have only ourselves to blame. I don't want that to happen. So, let's celebrate being endowed with the Holy Spirit. And, "Do not get drunk on wine, which leads to debauchery. Instead, let each of us be filled with the Spirit" (Ephesians 5:18, NIV).

Who wouldn't want to grow in their obedience to the Holy Spirit? Because of our Faith and Trust In God, WE ARE obedient to the Holy Spirit (not to grieve or quench).The question is, "have we been obedient?" Are we behaving? Once we've accepted Christ and have received the Holy Spirit, He begins a work in us to transform us into the image of Christ (Romans 8:29, KJV), He who did no sin. It's impossible for us to **FOLLOW** Christ unless we are LED by the Holy Spirit. And the only way to be led by the Spirit is to be **FILLED** by the Spirit (Ephesians 5:18, KJV). The Holy Spirit will never force us to do anything, but only to guide us in everything. He's to help us along the way on our spiritual journey. If allowed He will teach, lead, guide, comfort and counsel us; and, He also intercedes (Romans 8:26, KJV) on our behalf. In John 16:13 (KJV), Jesus called the Holy Spirit "The HELPER," and said: "When He, the Spirit of truth is come, He will guide you into all truth." I'm a witness and I love the gospel song: ♪♫"The Comforter" by Edwin Hawkins Singers, 1977. Yes, He's our **GUIDE** and **COMFORTER**! We should also know that the Holy Spirit is co-equal with God the Father and God the Son and is of the same essence; The Godhead, The Trinity. Get to know them! ♪♫"It's Good To Know Jesus" (Mississippi Mass Choir). I don't know about yawl, but myself, I always need **HELP**er! Anyone else need **HELP**er? Ask? ♪♫"Holy Spirit, Come Fill This Place" (CeCe Winans)

Biblically, did you know that the Holy Spirit empowerment starts from Genesis to Revelation? Check it Out Yourself. In addition, that the Holy Spirit's involvement in the life, ministry, and mission of Jesus Christ is phenomenal! Being anointed with the Spirit and/or Endowed with His Power is also phenomenal! ... To be like Jesus! Check Him out for yourself!

Recently, while meditating in HIS presence; and reading the King James Versions of 1

Thessalonians 5:19 and Ephesians 4:30; I was counseled to, "Quench not the Spirit" And, "Not to Grieve the Holy Spirit." Being obedient and without hesitation, I began yielding to the Holy Spirit. He has given me this message to share with all reading - similar to what was also given to Jeremiah (Jeremiah 1:4 KJV), "Then the word of the Lord came unto me, saying..." *"I've known you before you knew me. I love you and I miss you. Numerous times, I've tried to get your attention, but you're so busy. If you have any time, can you please talk to me; before bed, before work, before eating, before traveling, or before making any decisions? And always remember Me, whether in good or bad times; during any or all circumstances, no matter what. I simply want you to surrender all and render all and to make me yours and you mine. I'd love to be one with you and I'm always available to you. I proved my love for you, when I gave my life for you. Most of you know and call me from one of many names. I AM available and listening; and, I pray you know my voice. I'm also praying you not just know of me; but get to know me. I AM truly yours, The Holy Spirit."* "He that hath an ear let him hear what the Spirit saith unto the churches." Amen.

I'd like to thank every reader for personally taking the time to acquire this book and read these Spiritual Messages. Being obedient, I was filled and led to spiritually construct every message. Just being Spiritually Obedient to my present calling. The Holy Spirit puts it on me, and I then filled, I lay it down to 'you' the readers. Yes, I put it on yawl! If allowed, the Holy Spirit will Convince, Comfort, Counsel, and Cleanse each of us. He also Intercedes, and Guides us, Retraining Evil. We should let Him have His way. I'm led to do my God-Thang, as you do yours. Just know it's impossible to follow God unless we are led by the Spirit. Not just any spirit, but The Holy Spirit! How can we tell if we're being led by the Spirit? We can tell by the "Fruit" of our life - our attitudes and actions (Galatians 5:22-23, KJV). It's the characteristics of God and it's God's Gift (The Holy Spirit) and the "Fruits" that enriches and blesses every area of our life; again, if we allow it. I have Faith in God and I believe in yawl, the recipients who are attentive in reading these messages. Thus, living the life as intended in God's Will. It is a life empowered by the Precious Holy Spirit. I Pray unto God that each of us (each of you) are filled and blessed by each message and filled with the Holy Spirit. God Bless All!

EPILOGUE

Yes, I physically wrote these Spiritual Messages but I was spiritually led to do so. I must say that it's not about me; it never has been because it's about He that is within me. I write because of Him. I write because there is a need... In Hosea 4:6 (KJV), it tells us that "God's people are being destroyed for lack of knowledge." Being obedient to the Holy Spirit, I'm grateful to have written this book with these uplifting spiritual messages. I am highly favored to have been chosen, shaped, molded and now responsible towards helping believers who want to grow in grace and in the knowledge of our Lord and Savior Jesus the Christ. (*I know I have some Soldiers out there like me.*) Every Sunday, denominational churches have members that are not being fed the word; in some instances, they are not being led by the Holy Spirit. They're not growing in grace. They don't grow they just idle. I've been in a church like that; maybe, some of you are still in that church...

Of course, this does not apply to every church. Some Ministers and Pastors do a God-Pleasing job with teaching their parishioners. Your personal and rhetorical comments on these writings will be well respected, and I will be conscious of them, and their worth. Maybe some of the following will occur: "These Spiritual Messages are too long for me to read." or, "Why does it have to be so many?" or, "These messages seems to constantly step on my toes and I hate it." or, "These Spiritual Messages are only for those babes in Christ and not me." or, "Do they have to be so deep and spiritual" or, "I don't need to read them, because I have my bible." or, "I don't need to read them because I'm saved." or, "I don't like to read." And so on... It's important for us to see and appraise things with their true value, with the eyes of Christ.

When we pray, we do not pray that God will spare us the hard work of rigorous spiritual reading and reflection. Ignoring spiritual uplifting can be one's greatest folly. God's Word is "Spiritually Discerned." With that said, let us strive to be spiritually discerned. And let us also strive to be spiritually mature. I'm a strong advocate for Spiritual Growth. No one should be forced to grow in Christ. It's our personal choice. I'm just a servant as many, and I thank all of you for acquiring this book and reading these Spiritual Messages. They are blessed and ordained by the Holy Spirit. Read, and let the Holy Spirit empower you with Knowledge, Wisdom and Understanding. To God be the Glory!

We as believers want to grow in the Lord. We want to learn, grow and know the Gospel, contrary to those who want to traditionally talk the gossip. My prayer is for all reading these messages Learn, Know, and Grow in the Word and to follow Christ, while being led by the Holy Spirit. Am I asking too much? Yawl continue being blessed and while you're at it, be a blessing to someone. I've done what I was spiritually led to do; write and complete this book. I've prayed and my prayers have been answered that you enjoyed what I've written and you have grown from it. And, continue to grow. Please, re-read the messages as many times as you need to be spiritually enlightened and empowered. Pray, and read again. It's very important that we begin **"Learning the Way, the Truth, and the Life."** Our Salvation depends on it. God bless you all!

Printed in the United States
By Bookmasters